ARCHBISHOP SIMON MEPHAM 1328-1333: A BOY AMONGST MEN

ARCHBISHOP SIMON MEPHAM 1328-1333: A BOY AMONGST MEN

Arms of Archbishop Mepham
Azure three bendlets or

Roy Martin Haines

Copyright © 2012 by Roy Martin Haines.

Library of Congress Control Number: 2011919416
ISBN: Hardcover   978-1-4653-0239-7
            Softcover   978-1-4653-0238-0
            Ebook   978-1-4653-0237-3

All rights reserved. No part of this book may be reproduced or transmitted in any form or by any means, electronic or mechanical, including photocopying, recording, or by any information storage and retrieval system, without permission in writing from the copyright owner.

This book was printed in the United States of America.

To order additional copies of this book, contact:
Xlibris Corporation
0-800-644-6988
www.XlibrisPublishing.co.uk
Orders@XlibrisPublishing.co.uk
302499

Contents

Preface vii
Acknowledgements ix
Abbreviations xi

Chapter 1:   Prelude: The Episcopate in Canterbury Province and Beyond 1
Chapter 2:   An Unknown Quantity: Immediate Predecessors,
             The New Archbishop and his Team 8
Chapter 3:   Political Involvement: Lancastrian Alliance 28
Chapter 4:   Some Provincial Problems 46
Chapter 5:   Provincial Councils and Convocations 59
Chapter 6   The Fatal Struggle with St. Augustine's, Canterbury 63
Chapter 7   Final Assessment 79

Appendix 1: Acta of Archbishop Mepham 1328-1333 87
Appendix 2: Mepham's Constitutions 1329[1] 102
Appendix 3: Convocations, Provincial Councils and
             Other Ecclesiastical Assemblies 113
Appendix 4: Extracts from Canterbury Register Q 117
Appendix 5: Other Original Documents 124
Appendix 6: The Contemporary Episcopate 140
Bibliography 143
General Index 153

Preface

The registers of Archbishop Mepham and his successor Stratford were apparently lost, or more likely stolen, in the later Middle Ages. Stratford had been bishop of Winchester for some ten years, consequently much more is known about his activity in the episcopal office. Mepham by contrast is somewhat of an enigma. He came into office with an academic training in the wake of Walter Reynolds, who did not attend a university but was experienced in secular affairs and had been a confidant of the king when Prince of Wales. Unusually Mepham was elected by the Christ Church chapter and not provided by the pope. Bereft of political experience, he was unlucky in the time of his promotion, a period of struggle between the Mortimer/Isabella and Lancastrian factions, with the young Edward III a pawn, virtually powerless to influence events. It was only towards the end of 1330 that the king came into his own thanks to a coup d'état. Thereafter Mepham's attempts to exert his metropolitan authority and his lack of wisdom in avoiding conflict led to his sad denouement.

Fortunately we know quite a lot about his more combative activities thanks to the chroniclers, particularly Dene, the reputed author of the Historia Roffensis, and the St. Augustine's chronicler Thorne. In the eighteenth century Ducarel collected a large number of documents relating to the archiepiscopates of Mepham and Stratford, while others have come to light with the publication of the episcopal registers of his contemporaries. In 1997 my article 'An Innocent Abroad: The Career of Simon Mepham, Archbishop of Canterbury 1328-1333', was published in the English Historical Review. 'The Release of Ornaments in the Archbishop's chapel and some other arrangements following Simon Mepham's elevation', appeared in Archaeologia Cantiana in 2002. Since that time I have examined the Canterbury Act Books relative to that period and prepared an edition of Stratford's Winchester register, which has made it possible considerably to expand the study of Mepham.

R.M.H. Clare Hall, Cambridge.

Acknowledgements

As usual I have been grateful to the Society of Antiquaries for the loan of books and for copies of relevant items. The library of the Somerset Archaeological and Natural History Society has proved invaluable, and I am particularly indebted to its former librarian David Bromwich. The Canterbury Cathedral Archives furnished me with a substantial amount of material and recently supplied excellent digital copies of the Audience Court Books; a great advance on earlier methods of reproduction. The many other manuscript sources are acknowledged in the bibliography.

The substance of my English Historical Review article (1997) has been incorporated, as has the basic text of that in Archaeologia Cantiana (2002).

Abbreviations

Arch. Cant.	*Archaeologia Cantiana*
BRHE	*Bibliothèque de la Revue d'histoire ecclésiastique*
CCA Canterbury	Cathedral Archives
Councils and Synods II	*Councils and Synods II*, ed. F.M. Powicke and C.R. Cheney, 2 vols. (Oxford, 1964)
CPL	Calendar of Papal Letters
CPR	Calendar of Patent Rolls
D.C.L.	Doctor of Civil Law
D.Cn.L.	Doctor of Canon Law
D.Th.	Doctor of Theology
DUDP	Durham University Department of Palaeography

EA.	R.M. Haines, *Ecclesia anglicana: Studies in the English Church of the Later Middle Ages*, Toronto
EETS	*Early English Text Society*
EHR	*English Historical Review*
HR	Historia Roffensis
JEH	*Journal of Ecclesiastical History*
Le Neve	*John le Neve. Fasti Ecclesiae Anglicanae 1300-1541*, 12 vols Institute of Historical Research (London 1962-7)
Lic.Th.	Licentiate in Theology
Lit. Cant.	*Literae Cantuarienses*, ed. J. B. Sheppard, 3 vols. (Rolls Ser. 1887-1889).
M.	Magister
NRO	Norfolk Record Office
O.Can.S.A.	Order of Canons of St. Augustine
O.P.	Order of Preachers
ODNB	*Oxford Dictionary of National Biography*
Premonst.	Premonstratensian Canons

Win.R.S.	Winchester Register Stratford. See Bibliography s.v. Hampshire Record Office
Worc. Admin.	R.M. Haines, *The Administration of the Diocese of Worcester in the First Half of the Fourteenth Century*, London

Canterbury Cathedral 1817, from Dugdale's Monasticon

Chapter One

PRELUDE: THE EPISCOPATE IN CANTERBURY PROVINCE AND BEYOND

BISHOPRICS IN CANTERBURY PROVINCE

By Lanfranc's time—he was archbishop 1070-89—there were fifteen bishoprics in England.[1] Two more were to follow. It was Henry I who established the bishopric of Ely. At a council held at London in 1108 it was decided to carve it out of the over-populous and certainly over-extensive Lincoln. Hervey, bishop of Bangor, whom the king had put in charge of the Benedictine house at Ely following the abbot's death, was sent to secure confirmation at Rome, where he was made the first bishop. In 1109 at a further council at Nottingham the arrangement was ratified.[2] The last see to be created in the medieval period was that of Carlisle in 1133, though its continuous existence was not assured until much later.[3] Canterbury province thus comprised seventeen dioceses and four more in Wales, while York, admittedly the largest diocese in the kingdom had only two suffragans, Durham and Carlisle. With the exception of Galloway (Whithorn or *Candida Casa*), York's claim to metropolitan jurisdiction over Scottish sees ended in 1192, when Scotland was recognised as a separate province, but without an archbishop. Only in 1472 did St. Andrews became an archbishopric.

BISHOPS AND REFORM: THE THIRTEENTH CENTURY AND BEYOND

The Lateran decrees of 1179 (Alexander III) and 1215 (Innocent III) provided the basis of the reforms enforced by the episcopate during the reign of Henry III—the period chosen by Gibbs and Lang for examination—and subsequently.[5] During the interval between the Fourth Lateran Council 1215 and the end of Henry's reign in 1272 three sets of Canterbury provincial canons are recorded, while bishops of the province issued twenty-one sets of diocesan constitutions. Bishops of the province of York promulgated two more, one of which was a reissue by Richard Poore for Durham diocese of his Salisbury statutes. There were some notable legislators, such as Archbishops Langton and Boniface of Savoy, and conspicuously among the suffragan bishops, Robert Grosseteste of Lincoln. Such legislation remained in force and was subsequently added to or reiterated. Fortunately all is now available in a modern scholarly edition.[6] Thus by the beginning of the fourteenth century, our point of departure, both the structure and legislation of the *Ecclesia Anglicana* were firmly in place. All that remained to be done was to disseminate the legislation, to enforce it, and to add to it where necessary.

Another feature of this reforming period was the number of graduate bishops. These were in a position to spearhead the movement for reform, and not only by the issue of supplementary constitutions.[8] In an analysis of bishops of English sees during the period 1215-72 forty of them are categorized as 'university graduates and teachers', forty-two as 'administrators and magnates'—fourteen of whom were *magistri*. Eight of the bishops were 'monks,' while thirty-seven are classified as 'diocesan and cathedral clergy'—twenty-eight of them *magistri*.

Archbishop Simon Mepham 1328-1333: A Boy Amongst Men

The trend towards university-educated bishops was certainly sustained in the fourteenth century. During Edward II's reign and the regency of his son, the years 1307-30, the bishops can be roughly categorised as indicated in the following figure.

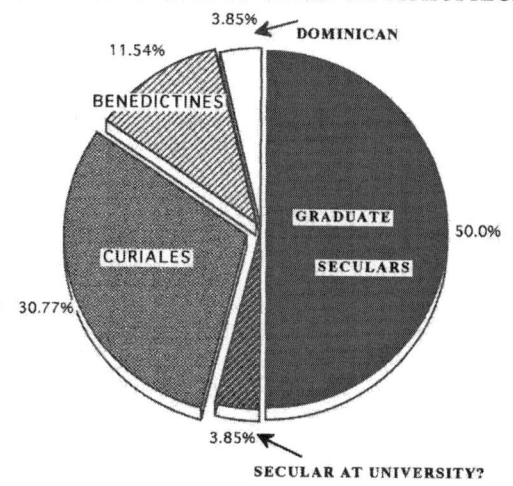

CATEGORIES OF APPOINTEES TO BISHOPRICS

- DOMINICAN: 3.85%
- BENEDICTINES: 11.54%
- CURIALES: 30.77%
- SECULAR AT UNIVERSITY?: 3.85%
- GRADUATE SECULARS: 50.0%

It needs to be remembered that sometimes bishops were not confined to a single category and that it would be an over-simplification to regard *curiales* merely as government hacks. A considerable number of them had taken degrees, particularly in law. Noble bishops were comparatively rare but regulars, despite the

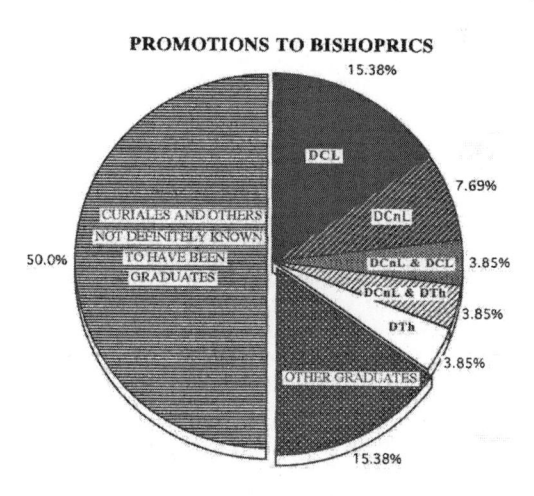

PROMOTIONS TO BISHOPRICS

- DCL: 15.38%
- DCnL: 7.69%
- DCnL & DCL: 3.85%
- DCnL & DTh: 3.85%
- DTh: 3.85%
- OTHER GRADUATES: 15.38%
- CURIALES AND OTHERS NOT DEFINITELY KNOWN TO HAVE BEEN GRADUATES: 50.0%

difficulties encountered by sees with monastic chapters to secure the promotions from among their number, managed to maintain a significant percentage.

Archbishops of the earlier fourteenth century also continued the work of legislation, though on a smaller scale. Thus the canonist William Lyndwood glossed constitutions attributed to Archbishops Robert Winchelsey, Walter Reynolds, Simon Mepham and John Stratford, men of widely divergent character.[11] However, the constitutions of 1322 attributed to Reynolds do not seem to have been originated by the archbishop. This and other attributions have been examined critically by Professor Cheney.[12] But we are on firm ground with respect to the constitutions of Mepham and Stratford, copies of which appear in contemporary documents. Mepham's legislation will be examined subsequently.

What Mepham inherited was a province in which some half of the bishops were university graduates. If we look more particularly at the situation during his archiepiscopate, we find that there were twenty-three bishops in office throughout England and Wales. Of these fifteen held English sees, four Welsh ones, while four more occupied sees in the northern province of York. For practical purposes John de Kirkby (Carlisle, 1332-52) can be largely disregarded, since he succeeded John Ross shortly before Mepham's death. Some bishops, notably John Droxford (Bath and Wells, 1309-29), John Hothum (Ely, 1316-37), Henry Burghersh (Lincoln, 1320-40), Stephen Gravesend (London, 1319-38), Hamo de Hethe or Hythe (Rochester, 1319-52), Roger Martival (Salisbury, 1315-30), Dafydd ap Bleddyn (St. Asaph. 1315-46), William Melton (York, 1317-40), and Louis de Beaumont (Durham, 1317-33), were already veteran occupants of their sees when the new metropolitan arrived on the scene. Some of them, such as Hethe, doubtless regarded him as an inexperienced newcomer. Only three bishops came from families of long-established noble rank: John Grandisson (Exeter, 1327-69), Burghersh, and Beaumont. Whereas the first two were well qualified in other respects, Beaumont, Queen Isabella's protégé, was clearly not, though whether he was as ignorant as some chroniclers considered him to be is a matter of opinion. Because of the growth of papal provision, supplemented by translation, not infrequently in accordance with the wishes of the government of the day, as few as three regular clergy secured election by their chapters: Hethe, a Benedictine, at Rochester; John de Eaglescliff, a Dominican, at Llandaff; and Kirkby, an Augustinian canon, at Carlisle. Those without degrees who rose to prominence through their training in government departments, frequently designated *curiales*, were Droxford, John Langton, Roger Northburgh, William Ayrminne, and William Melton, while Robert Wyville, despite his reputed ignorance, was another bishop advanced under the aegis of Queen Isabella, following early experience in her household. These details can be illustrated graphically as follows.

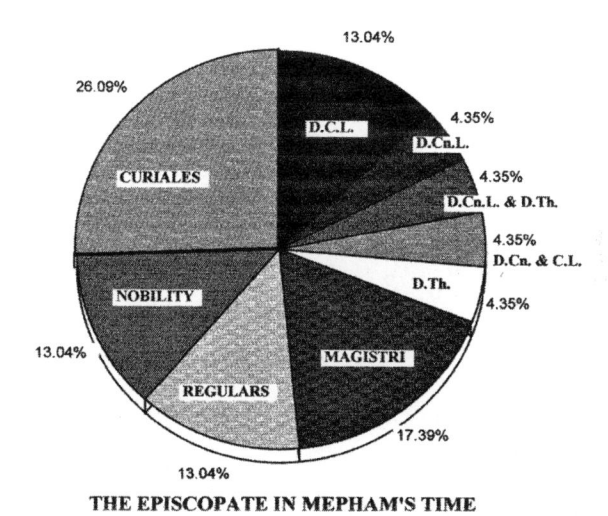

THE EPISCOPATE IN MEPHAM'S TIME

- 13.04% D.C.L.
- 4.35% D.Cn.L.
- 4.35% D.Cn.L. & D.Th.
- 4.35% D.Cn. & C.L.
- 4.35% D.Th.
- 17.39% MAGISTRI
- 13.04% REGULARS
- 13.04% NOBILITY
- 26.09% CURIALES

Surprisingly little is known about some of the bishops, in particular the Welsh ones, apart from Gower. Inevitably a number of the *curiales* advanced to high offices of state, but were joined by others with different backgrounds. The first four treasurers of Edward III's reign were John Stratford, Adam Orleton, Henry Burghersh, and Thomas Charlton, while John Hothum, Henry Burghersh and John Stratford were chancellors during roughly the same period. A number of bishops, notably Stratford, Orleton, and Melton were involved in politics at this time, but Mepham's efforts in this sphere, as will appear, soon left him isolated from the bench of bishops.

Endnotes

1. For Lanfranc's attitude as metropolitan see Barlow, 'A View of Archbishop Lanfranc', pp. 172-3, also by the same author, *The English Church 1066-1154*.
2. Miller, *Abbey and Bishopric of Ely*, p. 75. As he points out, Bentham, *History of the church of Ely*, printed the relevant documents.
3. Thompson, *English Clergy*, p. 40 and n.1.
4. For a concise summary of the confused Scottish situation with references see *HBC*, pp. 300-1, and for detailed treatment, *Series Episcoporum Scoticana*. In DUDP Reg. 2, fo. 109r, is a memorandum of a papal grant for the duration of the schism to Bishop William Skirlaw of Durham (1388-1406) of jurisdiction (*spiritualem et diocesanam*) over all persons subject to the English king within the diocese of St. Andrews.
5. Gibbs and Lang, *Bishops and Reform*. This remains an extremely important study.
6. *Councils & Synods II*, replacing the *Concilia* of Wilkins, the corresponding work of Spelman, and the texts in Lyndwood, *Provinciale*.
7. The recent work by Professor Helmholz, volume 1 of the *Oxford History of the Laws of England*, provides a fine survey of Canon Law from 597 to the 1640s.
8. Gibbs and Lang, *Bishops and Reform*, App. B.
9. Ibid. App. C. Some bishops are listed in more than one category.
10. This figure is included in my article 'The Episcopate during the Reign of Edward II and the Regency of Mortimer and Isabella', which includes much detailed information and an analysis of the involvement of bishops in national affairs. *Ibid*. App. I-2.
11. John Stratford's provincial constitutions are discussed in Haines, *John Stratford*, pp. 394-405. Salisbury Reg. Wyville 1, fos. 128^r-131^v embodies a text the rubrics for which are collated with those in Wilkins, *Concilia* 2, pp. 702-9, and BL Cotton MS Vitellius A.ii. *Ibid*. App. 4, where Lyndwood's glosses are also detailed. More recently, and without mentioning the above, Bray, *Records of Convocation III*, pp. 181-219, has examined the evidence for Stratford's legislation and printed texts of two sets of constitutions: an initial draft at pp. 187-99, and a second set at pp. 203-19, dated 25 October 1342.

[12] Wright, *Reynolds*, pp. 260-1; Haines, *John Stratford*, p. 395 and n.4; Cheney, *Medieval Texts*, pp. 169-71. and the discussion of texts in *Councils & Synods* 2, p. 1387. The 1322 convocation is examined by Bray, *Records of Convocation*, pp. 55-63, without mention of the attributed legislation.

[13] See App. 6.

Chapter Two

AN UNKNOWN QUANTITY: IMMEDIATE PREDECESSORS, THE NEW ARCHBISHOP AND HIS TEAM

CANTERBURY ARCHBISHOPS

Simon Mepham was an unusual, certainly an unheralded occupant of the metropolitan see, an important one in the European context.[1] His origins seem to have been semi-rural and relatively humble. Certainly he lacked influential patrons to further his earlier career, since at the time of his promotion he had accumulated few benefices. Moreover, he was a doctor of theology when there was a marked tendency for future bishops to incept in canon or civil law, a development favoured by Pope John XXII (1316-1334), himself a lawyer, and continued into the next century.[2] Thomas de Cobham, rejected in favour of Walter Reynolds (1313-27)—who lacked a university education but was not as unlettered as most chroniclers suggest—was a doctor of Canon Law and widely respected academically. Stratford, Mepham's successor as archbishop (1333-48), was a doctor of Civil Law, as was John de Offord who died in 1349 prior to consecration. Wincheslsey trained as a theologian, while Thomas de

Bradwardine, who succeeded John de Offord, was a particularly notable one, as well as being a mathematician. In fact he has been described by a biographer as 'one of the central thinkers of the fourteenth century',[3] but he like Offord died in 1349, just over two months after consecration. No other theologian was to occupy the see of Canterbury during the remainder of the fourteenth century.

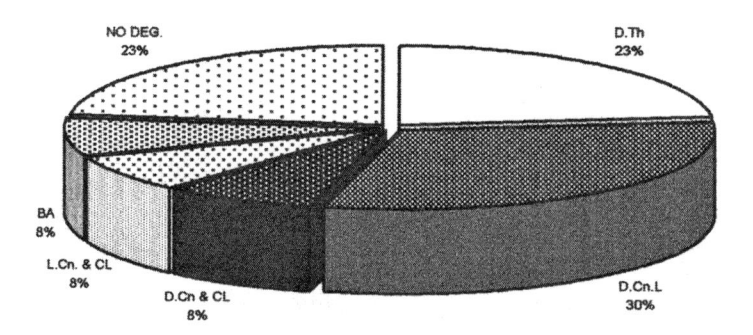

CANTERBURY ARCHBISHOPS: DEGREES

- NO DEG. 23%
- D.Th 23%
- BA 8%
- L.Cn. & CL 8%
- D.Cn & CL 8%
- D.Cn.L 30%

Of the thirteen archbishops of the southern province during that half century all but three had degrees. One of these three, Simon Langham, a Benedictine, had begun to study at Oxford, possibly theology.[4] The various disciplines are illustrated by the following diagram. As will be seen, almost 50% of the archbishops were lawyers.

EARLY YEARS: FAMILY CONNECTIONS, EDUCATION

Only an estimate of the date of Mepham's birth can be made, nothing unusual at this time: it was probably somewhere in the mid-1270s. Everything points to his having been born and brought up at his nameplace in Kent some five miles south of Gravesend on the Thames Estuary. Meopham, though in Rochester diocese, lay within the immediate jurisdiction of the archbishops. The family owned some property in the area and his parents were buried in the church or churchyard.[5] Two brothers appear not infrequently in the records: Simon and Edmund. The latter followed a similar academic career at Oxford and is first mentioned as a doctor of theology at the same time as the future archbishop. Both were to hold canonries at Chichester. Edmund became rector of Brasted and in 1314 received a dispensation to be absent from his benefice for the purposes of study as well as licence to choose his own confessor. In 1327 he was a prebendary of Llandaff. Brasted was to be his final resting place.[6] His monumental brass in that church, now merely an indent, bore the date 1333.[7] If that is accurate, as must surely be the case, the Pauline annalist is mistaken in stating that Edmund was mortally ill in 1328 when his brother, newly elected archbishop, rushed from Lynn to London allegedly on that account. However, a crossed-out entry in Mepham's Audience Court Book, undated but almost certainly from 1329, records Robert Leueye acting as an executor of a M. Edmund de Mepham.

Brasted Church, Kent.
Indent of Edmund de Mepham's lost brass, 1333.

Another brother, Thomas, was a regular clerk, his Order apparently unknown. A sister, Joan, married John de la Dene a local man of substance who with the brothers Simon and Edmund Mepham secured licence in 1327 to alienate a messuage, mills, land, and rent in Meopham and nearby East Malling, Birling,

Northfleet, Meopham and Hoo for the endowment of a chantry in the chapel of St. James de la Dene within the parish of Meopham for the souls of the founders, of Joan de la Dene, and of their parents relations and benefactors. A transcript of the substance of this licence is given by Golding-Bird, Meopham's historian, who summarises the results of the *Inquisitio ad quod damnum*.[9] The document is strangely imprecise, but the author argues that this chapel was within the church itself, probably in the earlier lady chapel. Although this is likely, the evidence cited is hardly conclusive. The reconstruction of the church, licence for the re-dedication of which had been issued by Archbishop Reynolds on 14 May 1325, was probably still incomplete, so the indulgence was clearly directed towards its completion and furnishing.[10] In July 1329 Simon was to issue a forty-days' indulgence for those visiting the church and praying for the souls of his parents, but not, it may be noted, of that of his brother Edmund, or even for his well-being.[11] A M. Richard de Mepham, of an earlier generation, was a supporter of Simon de Montfort, but that the future archbishop was likewise christened Simon must surely be a coincidence.[12] Yet another namesake, M. William de Mepham, roughly contemporary with the archbishop, was a canon of Salisbury, but not accounted an Oxford graduate by Emden. At present there is no evidence of his connection with the archbishop's family.

Remarkably little can be gleaned about Simon's early career. He seems to have studied at Oxford, becoming *magister* by 1295. In that year he was collated to a canonry of Llandaff and ordained acolyte by Archbishop Winchelsey. He proceeded to the priesthood two years later, 21 September 1297, by which time he was rector of Tunstall in Kent, a benefice he retained until his promotion to the archiepiscopate. It would seem, *pace* Emden, that he could not have been the archdeacon of Salop in Coventry & Lichfield diocese, described as *magister*, whom Bishop Langton, Edward I's chancellor, despatched in February 1299 on an unsuccessful mission to Bishop Swinfield of Hereford. The purpose of this mission is unknown, but Swinfield's written response was that he could go no further than the obligations ordinarily accepted by the bishops, and had explained this *viva voce* to the archdeacon. Presumably Langton was requesting financial support for the king.[14] This Simon is clearly the man named in a royal writ of 12 February 1330 entered in Bishop Burghersh of Lincoln's register. The writ required the distraint of M. Simon de Mepham, rector of *Newenham* (Nuneham), an executor of a M. Simon de Mepham, deceased, sometime archdeacon of Salop, to appear before the barons of the Exchequer at Westminster in fifteen days of Easter. There he was to respond for the issues of the lands of alien religious in the Isle of Wight, taken into King Edward I's hand by reason of the war with France, and which had been held as custodian by the senior M. Simon.[15] Clearly we have here two further men of the same name, at least one of whom died during Mepham's archiepiscopate. Both may well have been the archbishop's relatives.

The future archbishop continued his studies in the theological faculty, in February 1314 securing a one-year licence of absence from his cure. The following year, entitled D.Th., he acted on a commission of Oxford theologians, including the then-chancellor Henry de Harclay, which condemned certain 'errors'.[16] In 1317 he had papal provision to a canonry of Chichester where he secured the prebend of Hova Villa. On his promotion in 1328 Edmund succeeded him there, likewise by papal provision.[17] Emden thought that the future archbishop was rector of Nuneham Courtenay, but as has been shown it was another Simon who held that benefice in 1330. On 24 December 1332 an entry in the Lincoln register of Bishop Burghersh records the admission of one M. John de Coleshull to Nuneham Courtenay at the presentation of Abingdon abbey. The vacancy is said to have been due to the institution of the last rector, a M. Simon de Mepham, to Brasted church in Kent. Yet Brasted was in Edmund de Mepham's possession from 1314 until his death in 1333.[18] Moreover, in view of Simon's promotion to Canterbury in 1328 this poses an insuperable problem. He cannot be the same man as Emden thought, despite the mode of address. There were in fact, as shown above, two other Simon de Mephams, also *magistri*, one of whom had died by 1330, which might help to make sense of a cryptic reference to an 'S. de Mepham' in the *Historia Roffensis*.[19] Be this as it may, up to 1328 there was nothing remarkable about the future archbishop's career; a degree of obscurity and certainly no pointer to his striking elevation.

A VACANCY AT CANTERBURY: MEPHAM'S ELECTION

The death of Walter Reynolds on 16 November 1327 at his manor of Mortlake precipitated an election at Canterbury at a time when political affairs remained in flux. Edward II—Edward of Caernarvon or, in the Welsh form Caernarfon, as he was entitled after his deposition—was not yet buried, rumours were rife, and the competing political factions were flexing their muscles. It was only recently at a council assembled at Stamford that Queen Isabella, who had fractured the matrimonial bond, had been under pressure publicly to clear her name.[20] There must have been government concern for a smooth succession at Canterbury and, above all, for someone who had not been a party to recent events, would not muddy the waters, and hopefully would remain politically innocuous.

Reynolds was buried on the Friday after the feast of St. Katherine the Virgin, that is 27 November 1327. The monks of Christ Church promptly despatched two monks, Brothers Walter de Norwyco and Simon de Sancto Petro to seek the king's licence to elect. This was granted on the 30th in the name of the young Edward III and was brought back to Canterbury on 7 December. The following day the royal letters were read out in chapter in the presence of two notaries and three witnesses. The 11th was then appointed for the election, when it was decided to proceed by way of compromise. Three monks (Robert de Dover, Thomas de Greneweye and Richard de Oxenden—the future prior) were chosen to appoint seven compromisers. The choice of the seven fell unanimously (*concorditer*) on Simon de Mepham, whereupon Prior Eastry proclaimed the outcome.[21] On the 15th two monks, Geoffrey Poterel and Richard de Ickham, set off for Chichester, where the elect was a canon and prebendary of Hova Villa, to acquaint him with the chapter's decree of election. After the conventional show of reluctance

Mepham consented on the 21st. The envoys, together with the elect, travelled to the court at Lichfield which they reached on 2 January 1328 and presented the letters of the chapter and those of the elect to the juvenile king. Edward, doubtlesss under instruction, assented to the election on 5 January, graciously admitted it, and on the following day a letter was sent to the pope from Nottingham praising Mepham as a man bereft of worldly goods but replete with virtues.[22] Letters of the same date to the cardinals followed, together with others from the chapter to the pope. For Mepham's journey to the Curia letters of safe-conduct were issued and M. Edmund de Mepham and William de Fissheburn were meanwhile appointed his attorneys.[23] Poterel, now with another monk, Nicholas de Ivingho, acting as instructors, and another, John Everard, as proctor, set out with the elect on 17 January from Dover for the continent to seek Pope John XXII's confirmation. All three had been compromisers for the election.[24] That Everard expired in Brabant on the return journey and had to be buried at Antwerp, and that Poterel died at Chester two weeks thereafter could scarcely have been a good omen for the subsequent archiepiscopate.

The elect's journey to the Curia was in the nature of a precaution; capitular elections might be overridden by papal provision. The court was anxious for a speedy resolution of the matter and further letters to that effect were addressed to the Curia from Barlings near Lincoln.[26] Others followed in quick succession: one from Queen Isabella, in which she declared that were anyone else to be chosen it might give rise to scandal, even schism; another from the English magnates who blamed the inappropriate behaviour of the prelates for the country's recent divisions.[27] By April there was growing uncertainty at court about the lack of a positive response from the papacy and even a rumour that the pope might wish to translate Burghersh from Lincoln.[28] This pessimism, reiterated in another letter from Northampton on 10 May was to prove unfounded.

Quite why Mepham's name came to the fore and was so strongly supported may never be known. Maybe, remembering the jibes about Reynolds 'illiteracy',[30] the monastic chapter sought to redress the balance by electing a scholar; one who had the additional advantage of being a local man. The case of that archbishop manqué, the scholarly Thomas de Cobham, another local man, who in the event had to content himself with the bishopric of Worcester, was doubtless fresh in their minds.

There were able monks in the Christ Church chapter, but a regular was unlikely to be acceptable in a wider context. In any case, there was no recent precedent. Prior Adam de Chillenden had been elected in 1270, but had to resign at the Curia two years later when Robert Kilwardby was provided. The last regular clerk to be promoted to Canterbury was the Franciscan scholar John Pecham in 1279. Whether, following Reynolds's death, alternative candidates were seriously mooted has not transpired, but from the government's viewpoint controversy would have been anathema and hence, as we shall see, strenuous efforts were made to secure speedy confirmation of the election. It is possible that the name of Henry Burghersh, the bishop of Lincoln, was raised, as mentioned above. He had suffered persecution at the hands of Edward II, which he laments in his petition to the apostolic see in April 1327,[31] and was to remain loyal to Queen Isabella for the whole of her regency,[32] but his association with the recent struggles would have militated against his candidature.

On 27 May Mepham's election was confirmed by the pope and on 5 June he was consecrated at Avignon in the church of the Dominicans by the cardinal bishop of Palestrina, Pierre des Prés. On the fourth day following he received the pallium, considered to confer the plenitude of pontifical authority.[33] A papal bull requesting Edward III to receive Mepham favourably is dated 8 June.[34] On that day he became liable for the regular obligation of common services amounting to ten thousand florins, half of which was paid the following February, the other half in November, by the agency of the Bardi of Florence. He found it necessary to raise a loan of £2,000 sterling.[35] His financial position seems to have remained precarious for in December 1329 he issued a letter of obligation for repayment of a loan of £40 to the bishop of Chichester, John Langton.

A notarial document was drawn up on 19 June at Avignon attesting Mepham's commission to M. Edmund de Mepham to act as the archbishop's Official and vicar-general. The notary responsible was the Canterbury clerk, Simon de Charing, who was to be employed by Mepham's successor, John Stratford, while one of the witnesses was Thomas de Woghope (Wouhope), who seems to have travelled from England with the archbishop.[37] In July, as though anticipating the problems that soon materialised, he petitioned for remedy with respect to sentences which might be brought against him by delegates or judicial officers of the papal Curia involving penalties of excommunication, suspension or interdict for failure to execute mandates to the great scandal of his office.

Following his return journey through France the archbishop is said to have reached Brabant, where he embarked at Antwerp, making his landfall at Dover on 5 September, the feast of Abbot Bertinus.[39] Thence he journeyed by way of Chartham and Rochester to Gravesend, where he crossed the Thames en route to the north. Conceivably Mepham was at Canterbury on the 8th when various ecclesiastical ornaments were released by the sacrist of Canterbury to Woghope as warden of the archbishop's chapel in his palace.[40] The archbishop then journeyed to Norfolk where he performed fealty to the king at Lynn, the temporalities being restored the same day, 19 September. The previous day the king had presented a royal clerk to a prebend in South Malling by reason of the vacancy and sent a mandate in pursuance to the new archbishop, and on the day of the restoration presented one John de Crokford to Wittersham in Kent, on the same pretext. Mepham's enthronement was postponed, possibly because of the volatile political situation, but also due to the fact that, as will be shown, on earlier occasions the earl of Gloucester had acted as steward. Precedents were discussed with the veteran Henry de Eastry, who was ever ready to give advice, but no immediate decision was apparently taken.

Mepham suffered from a major disadvantage: he had scant experience of administration and of the contacts which that inevitably engendered. Winchelsey had had much experience in the Schools, though avoiding the controversies then rife among the mendicant friars. He became chancellor of Oxford University, but like Mepham lacked practical knowledge of royal or diocesan business. Reynolds, by contrast, came to Canterbury with a background in both spheres, as did John

Stratford. One advantage of having been a diocesan bishop was that you would have rubbed shoulders with well qualified men, *iuris periti*, accustomed to the routine of spiritual, administrative and judicial affairs. Such men could be relied upon to smooth the path of a new prelate.

Most archbishops would therefore expect to embark upon their duties with a quorum of clerks experienced in diocesan matters or at least schooled in administration, ecclesiastical, secular, or both. Mepham, as we have seen, had not been a diocesan bishop but like Winchelsey had moved in academic circles. The latter was fortunate in being able to join the ranks of like-minded bishops such as Antony Bek of Durham and Simon of Ghent, the Salisbury diocesan.[42] In this respect Mepham was not so fortunate, as will be seen; his activities as a metropolitan visitor, always a difficult area, were to sour his relationship with the comprovincial bishops. Reynolds relied not only upon contacts he had made in government service and at his former diocese of Worcester, although that diocese saw but little of him, as well as on his relations. Among the former were Benedict de Paston, his vicar-general and diocesan Official at Worcester, and M. William de Birston, archdeacon of Gloucester and his erstwhile commissary-general. Among the latter were Ralph de Windsor, termed *consanguineus*, and possibly John de Windsor.[43] Despite his local origins, the Rochester chronicler, presumably William Dene, treated Mepham's denouement unsympathetically when reporting the new archbishop's return from the Roman Curia and his passage through Rochester diocese on his way to perform fealty and to secure his temporalities. He records unhelpfully that he came with his two brothers, M. Edmund and Br. Thomas, who were seeking clerks and members for the archiepiscopal *familia*. They could find no one suitable and, he mockingly remarked, were seeking angels rather than men for the task.[44] This thrust should not be taken too seriously.

The *Registrum Actorum* of Mepham's Audience Court reveals that from the beginning he could call upon competent men, even though most of them have not left their mark elsewhere in the records. M. Thomas de Hockele or Hockley, the archbishop's chancellor, occurs frequently in the manuscript as hearing a variety of cases, either alone or in conjunction with others. M. Robert de Weston, inherited from an earlier period, regularly acted as an auditor of causes, and on one occasion is termed auditor-general (curie sue causarum et negociorum auditor generalis),[45] while a M. John de Renham appears less often in this role. M. Robert Brok or Brook first puts in an appearance as an auditor early in October 1329 but frequently thereafter. A commissary-general, M. Thomas of Canterbury, occurs in connection with an appeal against one of his definitive judgements. Peter of Corbavia, in evidence during Reynolds's archiepiscopate, known to have acted, at least on one occasion, as suffragan bishop for the celebration of orders, appears as an auditor in the court.[46] Most of these *magistri* are hard to trace elsewhere and certainly did not secure canonries as did so many other clerks involved in ecclesiastical administration. A Thomas de Hockley D.Th., does appear in Emden's biographical register of Oxford, where he is merely noted as a friend of Ralph of Shrewsbury, a contemporary bishop of Bath and Wells.[47] M. Laurence Fastolf, canon of St. Paul's, at one time Mepham's treasurer, is to be found numerous times in his court book, and is an entirely different case.[48] He was to become prominent in the *familia* of Mepham's successor, John Stratford, acting once more as auditor in his court, as an envoy to the Roman Curia, as well as a royal commissioner for the opening of parliament.

A more intransigent problem was the new archbishop's relationship with the prior of his cathedral church. Henry Eastry had been elected as long ago as 1285 and in Mepham's time was in his late eighties, dying in 1331 in the 92nd year of his age. Speaking with the voice of long experience he adopted an avuncular, but sometimes a more strident tone to the new recruit.[50] In May of 1328, somewhat impatiently, he wrote a private letter to say that it was highly unusual, not to say unheard of, for a suffragan bishop of the Canterbury province who had been consecrated by someone other than the archbishop, whether in the Roman curia or anywhere else, not to make personal profession to him as soon as possible after such consecration in accordance with an attached schedule used in the case of Bishop Grandisson—*mutatis mutandis*.[51] Much later, in April 1329, he suggested that Mepham might inform his chancellor and other members of the council appointed to conduct his affairs that it was not the practice for any bishop to consecrate chrism or celebrate orders in the cathedral church unless the prior and chapter had first been informed by the archbishop's letters. Nor was it appropriate to celebrate orders in the infirmary, thus disturbing the quiet of those there, especially when there were other more suitable places. Bearing in mind his zeal for the archbishop's honour he hoped he would not attempt this.[52] The context of this letter is not revealed, but we do know that at the end of November in the previous year Mepham had commissioned Br. Peter, bishop of Corbavia, to hold an ordination in the cathedral church at the next Embertide (17 December) for those monks presented by the precentor, as well as for beneficed clerks of the city, diocese, and immediate jurisdiction.[53] Another letter from the prior lectured the archbishop on the necessity to have wide and prudent councellors, skilled in both canon and civil law, acting in his court. He has some, but should have more. Mepham, as the prior's letter shows, reacted against these repeated criticisms.

The prior sounded another warning note in December 1328 when Mepham commissioned the abbot of Westminster, William de Curtlington, to examine the credentials of John of Cirencester for promotion by papal provision. Eastry required the abbot to stay his hand until the archbishop could be better informed of the rights of the cathedral prior to deal with such matters. Then, by a letter of 30 December, he proceeded to inform Mepham that his action prejudiced the prior's privileges and those of his church, and he was not going to withdraw his objection. It was, he concluded, unprecedented that an archbishop should commit his authority to an abbot or any other exempt person contrary to the apostolic privileges of the chapter and church of Canterbury.

Their relationship had more constructive moments. The archbishop sent his donzel (*domicellus*) to consult the prior about a range of matters in November 1328: whether Adam Orleton on his translation from Hereford to Worcester was under obligation to make a second profession to the archbishop; whether the king had the right to the promotion of a clerk on account of Mepham's preferment; was it necessary for him to meet the king at Eltham or its neighbourhood and offer him a present; and whether the form for the summoning of the council which he had submitted for consideration was suitable. The prior responded to each question in writing: no second profession was necessary in cases of translation; the practice of granting a benefice on promotion has been exacted, become regular, and is now regarded as customary, but it was *de facto* rather than *de iure*; as to Eltham, he should not be concerned unless the king chose to visit the church of Canterbury in person; lastly, all clerics of the province, exempt and non-exempt were to be summoned with the exception of royal clerks engaged in their business, so that the archbishop's draft, which he was returning, seemed to him appropriate, apart from the one interlinear addition he had made.

Prior Eastry died on 8 April 1331, his successor Richard de Oxenden being elected on 25 April of that year. In July the new prior wrote to Mepham with a series of requests. First of all he asked that the penitentiaries, the archbishop's appointees, should have their hands tied (*habeant manus ligatos*) when they came to consider absolution in cases concerning the three basic vows of the Benedictines: poverty, chastity and obedience. He then asked Mepham whether the feast of the Translation of St. Benedict should be celebrated, there being some dispute about this among the brethren. His last query concerned absolution of a woman whom he suspected had killed her unbaptised child. Would the archbishop commit to him the power of absolution should he find this appropriate in the circumstances?[57] In the ordinary course it lay with the archbishop to admit novices, but Prior Oxenden politely suggested that if Mepham were not available he could so on his behalf.[58] A surprising bureaucratic error followed the issue of letters dimissory at the prior's request. They were not deemed acceptable by the ordainer, Bishop Hethe of Rochester, so that the archbishop's chancellor had to be asked to reissue them.

In practice Mepham did fall foul of the royal rights of presentation in that he failed to present a royal clerk to the church of Maidstone by reason of the vacancy.[60] The same benefice was to entail the archbishop's temporary suspension from office by John XXII when he failed to admit Cardinal Annibaldo Gaetani da Ceccano, a papal provisor.[61] Another presentation, that of Robert Wyville the future bishop of Salisbury to the church of Mayfield, an archiepiscopal manor, was disputed by Mepham in the royal court, whereupon a prohibition against the proceedings was issued.[62] Then there was the matter of purchasing the crops which had been sown *sede vacante* on the episcopal manors. The king's butler, Richard de la Pole, was ordered to oversee the sale of corn and hay from the archbishop's manors in Kent, Middlesex, Surrey and Sussex, some of the proceeds from which were to be assigned for the repayment of his debts to the Bardi of Florence. The archbishop agreed to purchase them at a reasonable price.[63] For the time being, however, it was not such routine affairs but a developing political crisis that was to engage the archbishop's attention.

Endnotes

1. For the often strained relationship between archbishops of Canterbury and the English kings: Haines, 'Conflict in Government'.

2. For a discussion of this matter at a slightly earlier period see Edwards, 'Bishops and Learning'. Hereford had lawyer-bishops between 1317 and 1344, London between 1338 and 1404, Winchester between 1323 and 1345, Worcester between 1327 and 1333. Ely, however, did not have a lawyer-bishop until John Barnet in 1366 and Lincoln had only one, Thomas Bek (1341-7), during the reigns of Edward I and II. The position is somewhat clouded by the fact that Pope John made much use of translation, so that the lawyer Orleton appears in three sees, John Stratford in two.

3. G. Leff in his illuminating biography in the *ODNB*.

4. W. J. Dohar in his biography of Langham in *ODNB* points out that if Langham did study theology at Oxford 'he was one of only four abbots of Westminster to have done so'.

5. The indulgence mentioned below was for those who visited Mepham church and who made a circuit of the *cimiterium* or churchyard 'pro animabus parentum nostrorum... quorum corpora ibidem requiescunt humata'. *Registrum Roffense*, ii. p. 777.

6. Churchill, *Cant. Admin.* 1, pp. 116 n. 4, 127-8 n. 9, citing Cant. Reg. Reynolds, fo. 7^r; *Le Neve* xi, p. 30. A summary account of Edmund's remarkably parallel career is in Emden, *Biographical Register Oxon.*, ii. p. 1260. He seems to have been slightly older than Simon and his beneficial advancement is a mirror image of his brother's, except that there was never the chance of a bishopric.

7. Mill Stephenson, *Monumental Brasses*, p. 268: 'A fine indent at Brasted a floriated cross with large half effigy of a priest above and a marginal inscription in Lombardics to Edm. de Mepham, S.T.D., rector 1333'. This is illustrated in Ralph Griffin and Mill Stephenson, *Monumental Brasses remaining in Kent*, pl.4, with a description on p. 68. The Society of Antiquaries has a rubbing.

8. *Annales Paulini*, p. 342; CCA ChAnt/A/36ii, foot of p. 8.

9. TNA (PRO) C143/195/8. *Inquisitio ad quod damnum.*

10 *Cal. Pat. Rolls 1327-30*, p. 62. Golding-Bird, *Meopham*, pp. 271-2, provides a transcript of the substance of this licence and, at pp. 156-7, summarises the results of the *Inquisitio ad quod damnum*. Ibid., p. 46 (citing Canterbury Reg. Reynolds, fo. 135v). The patent roll calendar gives the site of the chantry as the chapel of St. James of la Dene in the parish church of Mepham.

11 *Registrum Roffense*, ii. p. 777. A copy of the original indulgence 'lately found' in the church was in the possession of the incumbent, Thomas Wright (1742-63). In 1997 Dr. M. Bateson of the Dean and Chapter Archives in Canterbury, provided this and other references. However, I was subsequently informed by the Centre for Kentish Studies, Maidstone, that the catalogue at Strood contains no mention of the original indulgence among the Meopham parish records housed there. It would seem that this indulgence is referred to in the colophon of the manuscript containing William de Shoreham's metrical work on the Seven Sacraments etc. He was vicar of Chart Sutton. See Wheeler, 'William de Shoreham', p. 154.

12 *Biog. Oxon.*, ii. pp. 1260-

13 *Le Neve* iii. pp. 31, 68, 79, 86.

14 *Hereford Register Swinfield*, p. 350. Philip de Cornubia was archdeacon by 1304, *Le Neve*, x. p. 17.

15 Lincoln Reg. Burghersh 4B, fo. 128^r. See n. 19 below.

16 These details are from Emden, *Biog. Oxon.*, ii. p. 1261, citing Winchelsey's published register; Canterbury Reg. Reynolds fo.10^r; *Munimenta. Acad. Oxon.* (Rolls Ser 1868) i. pp. 101-02. Three books given by Mepham to Canterbury Cathedral Priory passed respectively to Trinity College, Cambridge (TCC 133, Thomas Aquinas, 969 Bartholomew Anglicus), and Sion College, London (Arc. L.40/L2, Psalter etc.). Neil Ker, *Medieval Libraries*, pp. 32-3, 37, 241. 1314/15 was a crucial year. The body of the royal favourite Gaveston was 'translated' to Langley (2 January 1314/15) and Harclay was credited with preaching a sermon at Oxford which elsewhere is attributed to John Stratford. Lambeth MS 99, fo. 137^r; Hereford MS P. 5 xii. See Haines, 'Some Sermons at Hereford'.

17 *Le Neve*, vii. p.32; Emden, *Biographical Register Oxon.*, ii. p. 1261.

18 Lincoln Reg. Burghersh IV, fo. 265ᵛ: *Reg. Burghersh*, ii. no. 1819: Stow Park, 24 December 1332. This is indexed in the latter without comment.

19 HR fo. 53ᵛ: 'quia episcopus [Roffensis] magistros S. et E. de Mepham et eorum sorores et parentes ad se vocare noluit'. This, of course, is an unfriendly jibe directed at a novice who ostensibly wished to direct matters by means of a coterie of family members.

20 Haines, 'Stamford Council', provides the details.

21 EA, 2b 'The Election of Archbishops of Canterbury', esp. pp. 30-1; CCA ChAnt/S/392.

22 *Foedera* (Hague) 2 iii. pp. 4-5; (R.C.), 2 ii. 727. 'Magistrum Simonem de Mepham canonicum Cicestrensem sacre theologie doctorem, virum utique terrenis opibus pauperem, set virtutibus locupletem.'

23 *CPR 1327-30*, p.199.

24 CCA DCc Reg. Q, fos. 123ʳ-5ʳ; CCA ChAnt/C/231.

25 *BRECP*, pp. 155 (citing CCA Lit. Ms D.12, fo 16 for Everard's death and burial); 207-8 (s.v. Ikham, citing Lambeth MS. 243, fo. 5, re 'negotiations concerning the election of an abp'); 256-7 (s.v. Poterel).

26 CCA DCc Reg. Q, fo. 125ʳ; *Foedera* (Hague), 2 iii. pp. 8-9; (R.C.), 2 ii. pp. 737-8: Barlings 25 March 1328.

27 CCA DCc Reg. Q, fos. 125ᵛ-7ᵛ: 'Quot strages nobilium quot animarum et corporum pericula apud nos effluxisse retro diebus contigerint . . . ob quorundam Anglie prelatorum incuriam et regimen indiscretum.' This could be described as a partisan opinion in view of the nobility's own conduct! Phrases in this letter mirror those in that of Isabella.

28 Ibid. fo. 126ʳ⁻ᵛ (without dating clause); *Foedera* (R.C.), 2 ii. p. 739, Oundle 20 April 1328. 'Quod de confirmatione electionis praemissae, propter defectus aliquos, in ipsius examinatione repertos, verisimiliter desperatur, et quod de provisione ejusdem ecclesiae vestra paternitas ordinare proponit ista vice'.

29 *Foedera* (R.C.), 2. ii. p. 742.

30 This matter is discussed by J. R. Wright, in 'The Supposed Illiteracy of Archbishop Walter Reynolds'.

31 Reg. Aven. fos. 294ʳ-5ʳ, Avignon 15 April 1327. 'Nullam habet ecclesiam vel prebendam mense sue episcopalis usibus deputatam et quod idem Henricus retroactis temporibus quibus interdum per secularis potestatis abusum bona temporalia ad eandem mensam episcopalem spectancia sine causa fuerunt occupata in sua diocesi proprium locum non habuit in quo caput potuerit reclinare.' Much the same complaint was made by the bishop of Hereford, Adam Orleton, who secured translation to Worcester. Ibid. 31, fo. 217ᵛ.

32 HR, fo. 56v, mentions Burghersh as one of those in the queen's chamber in Nottingham Castle at the time of the audacious coup in October 1330. See also Baker, *Chronicon*, 45-6, notes 226-9 (extract from a version of the *Brut* chronicle in BL. Harley MS 2279).

33 CCA DCc Reg. Q, fo. 127v. 'Palleum, videlicet plenitudinem pontificalis officii, de corpore beati Petri sumptum recepit.'

34 TNA (PRO) SC7/56/19, 6 Ides June (8ᵗʰ)1328; *BRECP*, pp. 155, 256-7.

35 Lunt, *Financial Relations 1327-1354*, pp. 724-5; Rev. Aven. 30, fo. 443ᵛ-44ʳ; 36, fo. 538ᵛ. See Bibliography under Rome.

36 CCA ChAnt/A/36/ii, p. 8. Dated 28 December 1329 from his manor of Mortlake. It was a short-term loan though, being repayable the following 19 May 1330.

37 CCA DCc Reg. Q, fos. 129ʳ⁻ᵛ (see App. 4).

38 Reg. Aven. 31, fo. 122ᵛ, 14 July 1328, the same date as his papal indult with respect to visitation mentioned below.

39 TCC R.5. 41, fo. 128ᵛ (al. 129).

40 CCA DCc Reg. Q, fo. 130ʳ (App.4).

41 CCA DCc Reg. Q, fos. 123ʳ, 129ᵛ, 131ʳ; HR, fo. 51v; *CPL* ii, p. 272; *CPR 1327-30*, pp. 319-20. Other details are from *Le Neve* iv. p. 3, where the relevant references are given.

42 For a succinct account and assessment of Winchelsey's career see Denton's article in *ODNB* s.v.

43 Wright, *Reynolds*, pp. 62-3.

44 HR fo. 51ᵛ. 'In crastino Nativitatis Sancte Marie eodem anno [9 Sept. 1328] Symon archiepiscopus Cantuar' de Curia Romana veniens consecratus et per Roffam transiens pro fidelitate facienda et temporalibus recipiendis ad regem perexit [for peregit?]. Idem archiepiscopus et eius fratres magister Edmundus et frater Thomas de Mepham

nimium solicitantes pro clericis et familia ad serviendum sibi habendis, quia in toto regno Anglie ydoneum seu sufficientem ad eius obsequium invenire, angelos et non homines quesierunt ad hoc opus. Tandem tamen de familia nulli alteri convenienti se valavit quod exitus rei probavit.

45 CCA ChAnt/A/36/ii, p. 2. Weston is prominent in the earlier MS. CCA ChAnt/A/36/i.

46 CCA.ChAnt/A/36/ii. Six entries on p. 23 are linked by a line in the right-hand margin to his name and that of John de Renham as auditors.

47 *Biog. Oxon.* 2, p. 939, citing *Salopia* 1, p. 20 (*The Register of Ralph of Shrewsbury, Bishop of Bath and Wells, 1329-1363*, ed T.S. Holmes, Somerset Rec. Soc. 9,1896).

48 CCA ChAnt/A/36/ii, e.g. pp. 6-7, 9-10, 25, 28-31, 34, 37-8, 40-2. See also ChAnt/A/

49 *Archbishop Stratford*, pp. 93n, 116, 240, 385-6, 443, 456, 461,

50 There is an extensive summary of his career in *BRECP*, pp. 144-5.

51 *Lit. Cant.*, i. no. 276. The phrase 'Insolitum quidem est et inauditum' also appears elsewhere in the prior's correspondence with the archbishop.

52 Ibid., no. 275. It appears that an unnamed bishop had been commissioned by Mepham to celebrate orders in the monastic infirmary.

53 CCA DCc Reg. Q, fo. 130v. See App. 4.

54 *Lit. Cant.*, i. no. 290: 'De auditoribus causarum domini archiepiscopi et aliis'. According to the prior, Mepham was tired of being lectured: 'non placet vobis quod nos de cetero vobis scribamus vicibus iteratis, pro quovis remedio petendo super quibuscumque gravaminibus nobis illatis et inferendis; et ideo super hoc plangere cogimus, sicut orphani paterno praesidio destituti'. In November 1329 the prior made a specific complaint against the auditors of the archbishop's court, allegedly influenced by the master of Eastbridge hospital, in the matter of the poor sisters of St. James under the chapter's protection. Ibid. no. 284.

55 Ibid., nos. 261-2.

56 Ibid., no. 266: 'Vobis remitto, cum praeposteratione unius verbi interlinearis inter quintam et sextam lineam.'

57 Ibid., no. 359.

[58] Ibid., no. 375.
[59] Ibid., nos. 376-8.
[60] TNA (PRO), KB27/275, m. 12.
[61] Wright, *Reynolds*, p. 58 and n. 23; *CPL* ii, pp. 282, 299.
[62] *CPR 1327-30*, 28 Nov. 1328, pp. 341-2.
[63] Ibid., pp. 344, 355.

Chapter Three

POLITICAL INVOLVEMENT: LANCASTRIAN ALLIANCE

DEATH OF EDWARD OF CAERNARFON: A NEW REGIME

*M*epham's election coincided with the rule of Queen Isabella and Roger Mortimer during the minority of Edward III, that turbulent period in English history which followed Edward II's disastrous reign and deposition.[1] Bishop Hethe bemoaned the lawless state of affairs in all cities, towns and vills. In 1327 after celebrating Easter he retired to his manor of Halling n Kent where he built high walls round his courtyard towards the burial ground, a new larder and kitchen, and remained there the whole summer, autumn and winter until the Purification (2 February).[2] The bishop of Exeter, John Grandisson, made a similar plaint: in the manors of his bishopric damage had been perpetrated and items stolen.[3] They seemed to consider this state of affairs to be abnormal. In short, as an unknown quantity Mepham was precipitated into a cauldron seething with political, ecclesiastical, and social problems. Archbishop Walter Reynolds died on 16 November 1327, just when two irreconcilable national factions were emerging: on the one hand that of the queen and Roger Mortimer; on the other that of Henry, earl of Lancaster, the earls of Kent and Norfolk, the king's uncles, aided by Bishop John Stratford. Between the two, and virtually powerless, was their mutual creation, the youthful Edward III, who had yet to develop a separate following of his own. At or about the time of Edward's coronation an advisory council had been set up which is variously stated to have consisted of twelve or fourteen members, a number of whom were to be permanently at the king's side. Its effectiveness was of short duration: power passed inexorably to Isabella and her paramour, Mortimer.

Reynolds's death came some two months after that of Edward of Caernarfon, as the deposed Edward II was titled following the accession of his son. The captive Edward was reported to have died in Berkeley castle on the night of 21/22 September 1327. A month later his body was brought to the Benedictine abbey of St. Peter at Gloucester, where for some two months it lay in state until the magnificent funeral ceremony on 20 December.[5] The body of the king was interred beneath a Purbeck marble slab and in due course a magnificent tomb was raised above it. The king's alabaster effigy was placed on limestone slabs and an elaborate limestone canopy erected above it. The base has a Purbeck facing.

THE TOMB OF EDWARD II FOLLOWING REPAIRS
TO THE CANOPY SEPTEMBER 2008.

As far as Mepham was concerned this was all over and done with but, as will be shown, before his archiepiscopate had run half its course there were those who firmly believed that the former king remained alive and who acted upon that assumption. Rumour was to spread like wildfire and threaten to destabilise the government.

A NOVICE TRIES HIS HAND AT POLITICS

Mepham, despite or perhaps because of his political inexperience, soon launched himself into the political fray with the best of intentions. The prior of Canterbury, Henry Eastry, was still acting as custodian of the spiritualities in July 1328 when, in response to a royal mandate sent from Worcester, he directed the bishop of London, as dean of the province, to summon the bishops to a parliament at York on the last day of July. The earl of Lancaster declined to attend and Bishop Stratford returned that he had received the writ too late for execution.[7] Because of the earl's absence and that of other magnates and prelates business was declared to have been left unfinished, so another parliament was summoned to New Sarum (Salisbury) for 16 October.[8] Meanwhile the new archbishop, having performed fealty to the king at Lynn in Norfolk, arrived in London on 25 September, according to the Pauline annalist on his way to meet his dying brother.[9] The capital was seething with discontent. The Londoners were corresponding with Edward's uncle, the former king's half-brother, Edmund of Woodstock, earl of Kent, and with Lancaster. Sir Thomas Wake, son-in-law of Lancaster, and Bishop Stratford addressed the citizens at the Guildhall and are said to have broadcast their opinion that the king lacked proper counsel, which implies that the council set up at the time of the coronation was already defunct. On his way south the king, more importantly Mortimer and Isabella, learned that Lancaster was mobilising his forces at his principal seat, Higham Ferrers in Northamptonshire, at a time when Bishop Stratford is known to have been present.

These events were not propitious for the Salisbury parliament. For lack of a register we cannot follow Mepham's itinerary but it was not he but the keeper of the spiritualities who had been named in the writ of summons. Dene, though, claims that Archbishop Mepham was there and, being totally ignorant of the ways of men, adhered to the earls of Kent and Lancaster against the country's rulers, the queen (Isabella) and Roger Mortimer.[11] However, an entry in Bishop Burghersh's Lincoln register points to his having been in Suffolk on 28 October, in which case it is unlikely that he was in Salisbury for the parliament, except conceivably in its early stages. It was brought to a hasty conclusion at the end of October when, the Pauline annalist claims, archbishops and bishops and almost all the others withdrew in great confusion (*magna discordia*). Certainly Mortimer, who arrived with armed men and at this time was created an earl with the novel title 'of the March', appears to have dominated the session, although claiming that he intended no harm to the earl of Lancaster. The latter prudently kept his forces, strengthened by a contingent of Londoners, not far away at Winchester. John Stratford, Lancaster's mouthpiece at the parliament, fearing for his life, withdrew without leave under cover of darkness and is said to have sought refuge initially in the open countryside at Waltham Chase, then at his manor of Downton, and finally in his cathedral city of Winchester.[12] For this temerity the sheriff of Southampton (Hampshire) was ordered to see that he appeared before the king wherever he might be in the octave of St. Hilary. Stratford failed to put in an appearance, so the sheriff was then ordered to bring him before the court in the octave of the Purification (9 February 1329). The case was to drag on until the fall of Mortimer in 1330.[13] Doubtless this explains why Stratford is not recorded to have taken a noticeable part in the events immediately prior to the confrontation at Bedford described below.

The king accompanied by his queen, Philippa of Hainault, together with Mortimer, Isabella and members of the administration, travelled past the Lancastrian forces at Winchester on their way to London, where the Pauline annalist claims they were well received and showered with gifts.[14] No sooner had the royal party departed, moving westwards for safety towards the Mortimer lands in the Marches, than the Lancastrians arrived to be greeted with more genuine enthusiasm. Meanwhile a citation had been issued by the king's uncles, the earls of Kent and Norfolk (the Earl Marshal), urging attendance at an assembly in London a week before Christmas. They alleged that the king, contrary to Magna Carta and his own coronation oath, had been ravaging the countryside—conducting a chevauchée with an incalculable number of armed men and destroying his faithful subjects.[15] Bishop Hethe, who was recovering from a serious illness, was in receipt of his copy on the feast of St. Andrew, 30 November. He justifiably excused himself on account of his infirmity, but in any case had no intention of complying, preferring to prepare quietly for the Christmas festival at his manor of Trottiscliffe. Convalescence apart, he was keen to shun political involvement. The archbishop, banking on the special relationship of Canterbury with the see of Rochester, urged him to come to his support. Mepham was furious when the bishop sent him the reply he had made to the earls and began to say that Hethe had withdrawn himself from serious business, when one of his familia quipped that the bishop of Rochester wished to be an 'A' on his own. On hearing this the bishop retorted that he preferred to be an isolated 'A' rather than joined in syllables with the other letters, that is the bishops assembled in London. He marvelled that in the depth of winter the archbishop should choose to go to London from a distant location at the time of the Christmas festival to organise meetings behind the king's back with ignorant young hotheads (*cum iuvenibus et improvidis ac imperitis*).[16] Mepham, for his part, roundly denounced him as unco-operative. Certainly few bishops supported their metropolitan, possibly only those of London and Winchester, Stephen Gravesend and the politically active John Stratford, a consistent Lancastrian sympathiser, doubtless chagrined by the exclusion of the bishops from political decision making.

While these contentious happenings were in process Mepham on 29 November 1328 issued from Mayfield, Sussex, his summons to a provincial council at St. Paul's for the end of the following January. Its preamble dwells on the dangers of fratricidal strife and the evils already inflicted on the church, even to the injury, murder, and capture of ecclesiastics—Bishop Stapeldon's fate doubtless being foremost in his mind, particularly as the council was summoned to St. Paul's, the scene of his murder.[17] Chagrined by the exclusion of the bishops from political decision making, Mepham's solution was to muster the clergy in support of the Lancastrian 'reformist' programme.

EVENTS LEADING TO THE BEDFORD DÉBÂCLE

Warming to his adopted task, on 16 December from his Kentish manor of Otford, Mepham issued his mandate *Justus et misericors Dominus*, requiring processions for peace in church and realm and the settlement of dissensions. It was bolstered by the grant of forty days' indulgence. A letter of the same date is a scarcely veiled warning from Prior Eastry of the conduct expected of a metropolitan. He should hold to the middle way, as had the Mediator himself, remembering that after the king's person he was chiefly responsible for the conduct of the realm (*post personam Domini regis ad regimen regni estis principaliter obligatis*). Furthermore, he should deliberate with those who wish and can go forward rather than with those who are contrary (*prodesse et non obesse*).[19] This salutary advice fell on deaf ears. The 'conspirators' assembled at St. Paul's on the Sunday before Christmas (18 December). After the procession Mepham preached in the nave. Presumably this was an address designed to justify the assembly. At their meeting (*tractatus*) the Lancastrians determined to send the archbishop, the bishop of London, and the earls of Kent and Norfolk, the earl Marshal, to the king to dissuade him from riding around and seizing property from the church and people. In response a letter in the king's name was addressed to the mayor and sheriffs of London, in the hope of deterring them from lending support, above all armed support, to Lancaster and his adherents, as they had done earlier at Salisbury. A *pièce justificative* of royal policy—effectively that of Isabella and Mortimer—from the time of the unpopular treaty of Northampton with the Scots was sent from Gloucester, and this was duly published at the Guildhall. The Lancastrian barons Thomas Wake, William

Trussell, Thomas Roscelyn, and possibly Hugh Audley, were there to explain that Lancaster's reply would be made in due course.

A summary of grievances was drawn up, dated 21 December. This, among other things, reiterated the plaint that the king should have prelates and barons around him to provide counsel, reminded him of his coronation oath, of the need to observe customs granted by his predecessors, and urged him to refrain from making chevauchées in contravention of Magna Carta, illegally without the judgement of the peers (*par proces de ley et iuggement des piers*) and due sentence by the archbishops and bishops of the land. Mepham sent a copy to the court at Worcester together with an accompanying letter by the hand of the archdeacon of Essex, M. John de Elmham.[21] Lancaster himself spent Christmas in Essex at Waltham and did not come to the capital until the beginning of January.[22] The pro-Lancastrian, Knighton, describes how a great army including Hainaulters (*Wallanorum*) was being collected by Isabella, Roger Mortimer, and their adherents against Earl Henry, who did not consent to their evil activities (*eorum nefariis operibus*).

The government proceeded to publish its own ultimatum from the safety of Worcester on 29 December. The royal forces were to advance towards the Lancastrian heartland by way of Warwick and Leicester, which would be reached on 6 January. If the armed insurgents submitted before the 7th an amnesty would be granted, though this would not include the lords Beaumont, Roscelyn, Wither and Trussell. Knighton, the local chronicler, describes how the government forces reached Leicester on the 4th and spent eight days devastating and wantonly pillaging the area.[24] Lancaster's force was said to include the king's uncles—the earl marshal, Thomas of Brotherton earl of Norfolk, and the earl of Kent—the bishops of London, (Stephen Gravesend) and Winchester (John Stratford), the lords Wake, Lancaster's son-in-law, Beaumont, Audley, Roscelyn, and many others.[25] By mid-January the royal army was at Northampton and a version of the *Brut* chronicle gives a vivid picture of a nocturnal journey in the direction of Bedford, Queen Isabella clad in protective armour.

Archbishop Simon Mepham 1328-1333: A Boy Amongst Men

Armed with his instructions a confident Mepham advanced in the direction of Bedford, outstripping his companions, his cross and banner defiantly erect. As he approached the royal army, the archbishop paused to ask his attendant knight, Thomas de Aldon, whether he considered it appropriate for him to go forward and greet the king. Aldon, thought so, but with the provision that not a scintilla of his mission should be revealed. Were this to happen, he warned, the royal council would readily divine the whole truth and Mepham would be the subject of derision. But the archbishop, wrote Dene, was no Elijah.(2 Kings 1)—whose fire had consumed the king's soldiers; he lacked both the prophet's spiritual force and his moral worth. He duly greeted the young king and Queen Isabella, but once he had refreshed himself with drink, tired by the journey and his exertions, he waxed loquacious. The council listened to what he had to say and then responded with a defence of royal policy. Mepham was allegedly won over and sent back to his advancing friends with a promise of amnesty to all but four lords. All who had relied on him for peace rejoiced at his return, we are told, but on learning what had happened they soon changed their tune and began to pillory him.

Dene records that Mepham, not without obloquy, retraced his steps towards Canterbury for his enthronement. As for the earls and their adherents, they awaited the arrival of the king in confusion. He appeared mounted while they, on foot, prostrated themselves in deep mud to seek the king's grace. Their submission delivered verbally before the bishop of Lincoln was admitted under harsh conditions.[27] On 10 April Simon de Bereford, John le Mareschal and William de Kirkeby were assigned to enquire into the report that magnates and their adherents from various parts of the realm contrary to the statute of Northampton had come against the king with arms at Bedford and remained there for some time, committing homicides, robberies and other offences.

While Dene's account is at this point the most circumstantial it should be noted that Knighton, admittedly with strong Lancastrian sympathies, considered that it was the young king's uncles, Kent and Norfolk, who had betrayed Earl Henry, leaving him in the lurch. The archbishop he depicts as the author of an agreement to ensure that 'errors' would be rectified in the next parliament, thus avoiding a rising of the commons in Lancaster's cause.[29] In view of what had happened at Salisbury this must have appeared an unrealistic prospect. Murimuth has nothing to say about the Bedford affair itself, merely suggesting that the earls submitted to the king's grace at the archbishop's procuration.[30] This well-meaning but disastrous intervention in national politics was to be Mepham's last; without doubt he was out of his depth. For the remainder of his life he was to be engaged in ecclesiastical matters, only to find that they too could end in conflict and disaster.

Because of the date of his archiepiscopate and his known concern at this point with political matters, in particular with the behaviour of the royal forces as they advanced towards Bedford, it has been suggested that Mepham might have been responsible for the *Speculum regis*, a highly repetitive tract decrying the use of purveyance by the royal ministers and agents. Some manuscripts have ascribed it to Simon Islep, but because his archiepiscopate is rather too late Mepham, having the same Christian name, has been thought to be a better alternative. There is no evidence to support this view and it could be said that Mepham would have been chary of invoking further criticism of the king and his government. The late Leonard Boyle presented a convincing case for William of Pagula's authorship and this has been supported by the recent article by Cary J. Nederman.

The abbot of Ramsey, Simon of Eye, when summoning a Benedictine general chapter for 31 March 1329, seems to have been referring to the advent of the new archbishop and the young Edward III when he wrote of the Lord having provided most suitable leaders for both the ecclesiastical and secular arm, hence foreshadowing a more peaceful era. The timing is interesting because he was writing—20 February—immediately after the collapse of the Bedford insurrection, which he apparently assumed marked the end of the threat of civil war.[32] It can only be concluded that he was both unduly optimistic and out of touch with the underlying discontent which had temporarily gone underground.

Archbishop Simon Mepham 1328-1333: A Boy Amongst Men

ENTHRONEMENT

When a disconsolate Mepham returned to Canterbury immediate arrangements had to be made for his enthronement in the cathedral church on 22 January 1329, appropriately the feast of St. Vincent the martyr. Even here there were problems and the affair itself was distinctly low-key. Although many ordinary people gathered for the occasion, few magnates were present, William de Clinton, the future earl of Huntingdon, providing an exception. At the three previous enthronements—those of Reynolds, Winchelsey and Pecham—the king and the earls and barons of the whole realm had attended. On this occasion among prelates Dene enumerates only two bishops, London (Stephen Gravesend) and Rochester (Hamo de Hethe), also the abbot of Glastonbury and the prior of Canterbury, to whom the local abbots of Faversham, Langdon, and St. Radegund's by Dover, can be added. The Canterbury scribe permitted himself a rare comment on events: the king and a number of barons had promised the archbishop that they would be there but did not come because of dissension between them. No service was rendered in accordance with custom by Hugh de Audley for the barony of Tonbridge, or for the other fees. Because the prior of Canterbury had installed the last three archbishops, it was Prior Henry Eastry who claimed this right, rather than the bishop of London, who it was said, had been accustomed to exercise this office. Even the ensuing banquet was compromised. It was necessary to find a replacement for the earl of Gloucester, who by tradition acted as steward.[34] Gilbert de Clare had died at Bannockburn in 1314, without a male heir. A substitute had to be found. Mepham did not wish Hugh Audley, married to one of the Gloucester coheiresses and the current lord of Tonbridge, to which the *servicium* was attached, to perform it, possibly because of his association with the Lancastrian dissidents, but also because of his uncertain status in the matter. Audley was given a hundred marks but these were to be refunded if he were found to have no right. On the day of enthronement Sir Henry de Cobham was chosen by Mepham to perform the office. John de Mereworth was deputed to act as cupbearer *(de cuppa sua)*, Edmund Roger of Higham to serve food and drink at the archbishop's table *(ad serviendum in mensa sua de pane et cibo*). By virtue of the manor of Hatfield by Charing, the widowed Lady Badlesmere, who had defended Leeds Castle against Edward II, claimed the service of chamberlain—guarding the doors of the archbishop's chamber—but Mepham would have nothing from her.[35] The day after his enthronement Mepham exercised his right as titular head of the cathedral priory to remove certain obedientiaries from office and then retired to his manor of Teynham in Kent.

These much subdued festivities concluded the archbishop began his metropolitan duties by crowning the queen, Philippa of Hainault, at Westmnster Abbey on 18 February 1329. It was then high time to get down to other diocesan and metropolitan business: the provincial council was less than a week away and there were constitutions to be drawn up. Discussion of these will be postponed until Chapter 5. Despite the Rochester chronicler's derogatory comments Mepham had assembled a competent team and, as suggested in the previous chapter, inherited a number of able lawyers who practised in the Audience Court. Woghope or Wouhope became treasurer and an examining chaplain, together with Masters Stephen de Bosco and Thomas de Canterbury. M. John de Bloyou, formerly Official principal of Bishop Grandisson of Exeter, was appointed Official of the Court of Canterbury. Masters Robert de Weston, Laurence Fastolf and Robert Brok were all to be employed in the visitation of Rochester.[37] M. Thomas de Hockele, about whom little else is known, occurs as chancellor, as we have seen, while Weston is named auditor-general and Brok, Fastolf and M. John de Renham auditors. It is possible that Simon de Charing, who was involved from time to time with notarial business, was the archbishop's scribe of the acts. Woghope, rector of Smarden in Kent, and Fastolf, a canon of St. Paul's, were to be Mepham's executors, and the latter was to continue his career with Archbishop Stratford.

VISITATION

Mepham, having assembled his *familia* and held his provincial council, turned his attention to the visitation of his diocese of Canterbury. At the time

Archbishop Simon Mepham 1328-1333: A Boy Amongst Men

of his provision he had secured a faculty which enabled him to visit the dioceses of his province when he wished.[39] However, his primary visitation began, as was canonical, with the cathedral priory. On the first day of March 1329 he cited the chapter to appear before him on the morrow of St. Gregory (the 13th). The day before the prior had certified that all the relevant persons had been summoned for his visitation. In accordance with the recent papal directive *Debent*, and at the convent's request, the archbishop was accompanied in the chapter house by a minimal entourage: a single secular clerk, M. Robert de Weston, and a public notary, Simon de Charing.

The *dicta* or statements of the individual monks were then written down. This process occupied the remainder of Monday and most of the next day. On the ensuing Monday Mepham, armed with the *comperta* proceeded to correction in chapter. There were some denials, and purgation was ordered by a varying number of hands in accordance with the gravity of the offence. In the course of this procedure Mepham discovered that two monks had fallen under suspicion of wrongdoing and committed his authority to the prior for the imposition of purgations, which they failed to achieve. Eastry sent a personal letter to the archbishop which concerned one of the monks but by mischance it was left in Eastry church and was available for all to read. On that account he preferred to send a trusted messenger with a letter of credence. So far as we know the process was accomplished without friction and the archbishop was free to turn to visitation of the city and deanery of Canterbury.

On the Thursday after his corrections in chapter he began to visit Westbere deanery followed by all the other rural deaneries. At that point there is a lacuna in the record so we gain no idea of the thoroughness of the process.[41] However, his attempted visitation of St. Augustine's, Canterbury, was so disastrous and its ramifications so damaging to the archbishop that it must be deferred for separate consideration in the following chapter. As we shall see, Mepham's visitations of other dioceses in the province were to be a source of friction and in the case of Exeter even of armed conflict.

SOME OTHER PROBLEMS

For lack of a register only isolated instances concerning the archbishop and his diocese or province have come to light. One such is the complaint in a letter, dated 7 August 1329, that Edmund de Neville had used lay power to occupy the church of Great Horkesley in Essex, London diocese, thus preventing the rector, John de Coule, from gaining access to the church or its fruits. Mepham sought remedy by asking the king to instruct the sheriff of Essex to remove him.[42] Why it was the archbishop who took action and not the diocesan bishop, Stephen Gravesend, is not at present clear.

The relationship of ecclesiastical and lay authority is further illustrated by an indictment of a priest, Hugh de Burghton, before the Kentish justices, Henry de Cobham and John de Yfelde, for horse-stealing. He had been imprisoned and his goods confiscated but on his pleading innocence and successfully proceeding to purgation Mepham asked for his release to the church authorities and the restoration of his goods.

A third case concerns the archbishop's temporal possessions. He alleged that as a consequence of a charter granted to the Barons of the Cinq Ports in the first parliament of the reign (1327) there had been accroachments on his Kentish tenants to his disinheritance and that of his church. The petition for redress was endorsed with the order for the issue of a writ to prevent such accroachments in the future and to enable the archbishop to distrain his tenants for his services.[44] It is unlikely that much more can be gleaned.

Archbishop Simon Mepham 1328-1333: A Boy Amongst Men

Endnotes

1. Harding, 'The Regime of Isabella and Mortimer' (thesis); *Edward II*, chap. 7: 'The Iron Lady: Isabella Triumphant, 1326-1330', pp. 177-218; Ormrod, *Edward III*, pp. 1-7. The Rochester chronicler wrote *sub anno* 1327: 'Regnavit sic Rogerus de Mortuo Mari et regina imperavit circiter quatuor annos'. HR, fo. 50^v.

2. HR, fo. 50^v: 'per totum regnum in singulis civitatibus, burgis et villis malefactores dominabuntur'.

3. *Exeter Reg. Grandisson*, pp. 172-3 (no 30). A letter to Bishop Stratford asking him to denounce those thieves who had migrated to Winchester diocese. 'In maneriis episcopatus nostri Exoniensis muri, clausa, hostia, fenestre, et eorum ferramenta atque meremia, et in diversis officiis utensilia varia disrupta sunt enormiter et ablata'.

4. The first of the accusations against Roger Mortimer in 1330 was that after the Westminster parliament following Edward III's coronation four bishops, four earls and six barons should be close to the king to counsel him, four of whom: one bishop, one earl, and two barons, should always be there to give their assent to any important matter. This Mortimer disregarded (*nient eiant regard au dit assent*). Furthermore, after the Salisbury parliament Lancaster and other peers, allegedly because of danger and out of reverence for the king, had withdrawn to their own lands, lamenting that that they could not speak to the king or to counsel him as they ought. *Rot. Parl.*, ii. p. 52.

5. In 1307-8 Gloucester Cathedral commemorated the seven-hundredth anniversary of Edward II's accession. Many details of the varying views of Edward, his death, and his 'afterlife', have been collected by George Marchant in his pamphlet *Edward II in Gloucestershire*, (n.p. 2007), issued in aid of Edward II's tomb conservation project, now complete.

6. There is a detailed analysis of its construction in *The Tomb of Edward II*. Recently (2007) the canopy has been restored to coincide with the anniversary of Edward's accession and coronation in 1307. See previous note.

7. Winchester Reg. Stratford, fos. 38v-39r, edn. nos. 391-2.

8. Parry, *Parliaments*, p. 93.

9 *Annales Paulini*, p. 342.

10 WinRS, fo. 110r, edn. no. 1148, shows that Stratford was at Higham Ferrers on 13 Sept. 1328.

11 HR, fo. 51v: 'apud Sarum ubi archiepisopus Cant. novus modum et mores hominum totaliter ignorans comitibus Kancie et Lancastrie [et Lancastr' interlined] et eorum sequele qui contra reginam et Rogerum de Mortuo Mari regnantes sub colore utilitatis regni se partem facientes capit adherere.'

12 *Abp. Stratford*, pp. 196-7.

13 Parry, *Parliaments*, p.93; TNA (PRO), KB27/275/m.1^r /276, m. 9^v.

14 *Vitae Arch. Cant.*, p. 19. *Annales Paulini*, pp. 343-4. For these events and those immediately following see *Abp. Stratford*, pp.197-202, where the appropriate references are given. The main chronicle sources are HR, the *Annales Paulini*, the *Brut* chronicle (Harley MS. 2279) cited in Maunde Thompson's notes to Baker, *Chronicon*, pp. 218-20, and TCC R.5. 41, p. 127 (al.128)^v. See also Holmes, 'The Rebellion of the Earl of Lancaster, 1328-9'. The *Cal. P. & M.R.* of the City of London is particularly valuable.

15 HR, fo. 51v. 'Pro octo dies ante festum Natalis Domini predictum litteras comitum Kancie et Mareschall' recepit continentes quod omnibus aliis pretermissis Lond' veniret ad tractandum cum eis et prelatis super magnis periculis eminentibus regi et regno, eo quod rex in [cum?] multitudine armatorum innumerosa equitabat patriam devastando, res et bona ecclesie et regnicolarum contra magnam cartam et iuramentum in coronacione ipsius prestitum dirripiendo et capiendo.'

16 Ibid. fos. 51^v-52^r.

17 WinRS fo. 43r, edn. no. 441. 'Adhuc modernis temporibus carbonibus odii inter proceres reaccensis, maiora pericula et dispendia nisi deus advertat poterit verisimiliter formidare.' See also *Records of Convocation III*, pp. 101-3. The full text from the Winchester register is in App. 5 below. The previous archbishop, Reynolds, in a letter of 21 October 1326 had written to the Canterbury prior and chapter of his horror at the crime: 'tantus horror in cor nostrum ascendit, tantusque dolor undique nos invasit quod videbatur nobis animam nostram gladium pertransisse'. *HMCR Var. Coll.* 1, pp. 272-3.

18 Ibid.; *Annales Paulini*, p. 343.

[19] *Lit. Cant.*, i. 272.

[20] *Cal. P. & M.R.*, pp. 78-83; *Abp. Stratford*, pp. 201-2.

[21] CCA DCc Reg. I, fos. 427[r-v]: 'Supplicacio prelatorum comitum et baronum et tocius communitatis London[iensis] facta domino regi in festo Sancti Thome apostoli anno domini M°CCC[mo]xxviii. The text is printed in *Lit. Cant.* 3, pp. 414-6 from this source.

[22] *Ann. Paulini*, pp. 343-4; *Cal. P. & M.R.*, pp. 78-

[23] *Knighton* i. pp. 449-50.

[24] Ibid., p. 450: 'et spoliaverunt undique patriam, et boscos, parcos, vineas, stagna, piscinas, et secum abduxerunt quicquid preciosum aut vile manus eorum invenire poterunt, aurum, argentum, blada, utensilia, lectualia, mensualia, arma, vestimenta, bestas feras et domesticas, oves et boves, aucas, gallinas, et ornamenta ecclesiastica, nihil in ecclesiis inventum vel alibi relinquendo. ac si esset in tempore guerrae inter regna.'

[25] Stratford's itinerary, though thin at this juncture, does not support the claim that he travelled to the north with the Lancastrian army. He was at London for the preliminary meetings. Haines, *Abp. Stratford*, p. 481.

[26] *Cal. P.& M.R.*, pp. 85-6; CCC MS.174 (*Brut*), fo. 156v; HR, fo. 52r; *Knighton*, i. p. 450.

[27] HR fo. 52[v]. 'Recessit itaque archiepiscopus non sine magno scandalo versus Cant. vias suas direxit pro intronizacione sua facienda. Comites vero Lancastrie [et] Kancie et ceteri eis adherentes confusi, expectabunt adventum regis apud Bedeford ubi regi equitanti pedites occurrerunt et omnes in luto profundo genibus provolutis prostrati gracie regis se submiserunt, quod cuius graciam sub certa forma arta et dura faciente verbum episcopo Lincoln. [Burghersh] sunt recepti.'

[28] TNA (PRO), KB27/276/Rex m. 23[r]. A long list of names is appended.

[29] *Knighton* i. pp. 450-1 'Et fuit concordatum ibidem coram Simone archiepiscopo Cantuariensi et aliis episcopis et multis de magnatibus regni, quod omnes errores emendarentur in proximo parliamento sequenti; et hoc ne forte omnes surgerent communes in hac communi causa cum comite'.

[30] *Murimuth*, p. 58.

[31] Boyle, 'William of Pagula and the *Speculum Regis*'; Nederman, *ODNB s.v.* Pagula; R.N. Swanson, ibid. *s.v.* Islep [Islip].

32 Pantin, *Chapters* i. p. 208 and n. 8: 'Nunc Dominus in utroque brachio spirituali videlicet et temporali, aptissimum principatum ut videant omnes fines huius terre salutare suum, dum regno et sacerdocio discidia displicent...'

33 In BL MS. Claudius AV, fo. 41ʳ, the similarly optimistic scribe wrote of Edward III's coronation, 'Et sic post multos horrores nocturnos sol ortus est Anglis.'

34 There had been disagreement in the past about the earl's fee which Archbishop Reynolds tried to resolve by an indentured agreement, one part of which was to remain in Gilbert de Clare's wardrobe, the other with the archbishop's clerk, John de Ringwood. Cant. Reg. Reynolds, fo. 4ʳ. See also the enumeration of these fees in CCA DCc Reg. G, fos. 23ᵛ-4ʳ.

35 CCA DCc Reg. Q, fo. 134r-v.

36 For the archbishop's rights to make appointments in the priory, both initially (*cum primo ad capitulum declinaverit*) and on later occasions, see CCA DCc Reg. G, fo. 21.

37 *Reg. Hethe*, pp. 516-7, 520; *Reg. Grandisson*, pp. 180-1, 188 and index s.v. Bloyou; CCA DCc Reg. Q, fo. 129v; ChAnt/A36/ii. Churchill, *Cant. Admin.* ii. N: 'Tentative Lists of Office Holders', records only Bloyou from Mepham's time. Emden, *Biog. Oxon.* ii. p. 939, mentions a Thomas de Hockele D.Th. from the appropriate time, but it would have been unusual to have a chancellor trained in theology rather than law. He had connections with the bishop of Bath and Wells, Ralph of Shrewsbury. The Court book (CCA.ChAnt/A/36/ii) shows that a M. Thomas de Hockley was indeed chancellor. Conceivably there have been two men of the same name. See chapter 2 and *ibid.* n. 47.

38 Golding Bird, *Meopham*, citing 'a consistory court book', i.e. DCc ChAnt/A/ 36/ii, fo. 12. See also the earlier court book, DCc ChAnt/A/ 36/i and Appendix 5 below. For Laurence Fastolf see *Abp. Stratford*, index s.v. He was to serve that archbishop as a proctor in the Curia.

39 CCA DCc Reg. I, fos. 427ᵛ-8ʳ. It was regular practice for newly provided archbishops and bishops to secure benefits during their time at the Curia. See below p. 47 n.7.

40 Boniface VIII's constitution *Debent* was later incorporated in *Extrav. Commun.* 1, 7, c.1. Whether it was intended to be a general regulation, rather than particular to Durham,

was in question at Canterbury in 1325 and later: *Lit. Cant.* i., nos. 164, 301-2. See also *Worc. Admin.*, pp. 151-2.

[41] CCA DCc Reg. Q, fo. 134v; *Lit. Cant.* i., nos. 273, 274 *bis*, 275. The abandoned letter is intriguing and it appears that the monk in question was born in Eastry (*qui in parochia dicte ecclesiae de Estreia oriundus existit*). Some details of the judicial processes arising from the visitation are in DCc ChAnt/A/36/ii, fo. 6 et seq.

[42] TNA (PRO) SC8/236/11780.

[43] TNA (PRO) SC8/197/9806, 30 May 1330.

[44] TNA (PRO) SC8/97/48/40, undated.

Chapter Four

SOME PROVINCIAL PROBLEMS

THE CHRONICLERS' PERSPECTIVES

We would be even more in the dark about Mepham's activities as archbishop—due to the loss of his register,[1] probably at the same time as Stratford's—were it not for the information provided by two chroniclers: William Thorn or Thorne, a monk of St. Augustine's Abbey in Canterbury, and the author of the 'Historia Roffensis', probably William Dene, the archdeacon of Rochester.[2] Thorne's perspective is understandably skewed on account of Mepham's jurisdictional conflict with his house. He has nothing good to say of the archbishop. Dene also reproached the archbishop for his visitation of Rochester, but although he stigmatises Mepham as totally ignorant of men and of the realities of everyday life,[3] and as one who relied too much on his family connections, he demonstrates a measure of sympathy for his manifold misfortunes. In this he is perhaps reflecting the feelings of the central figure of his 'Historia Roffensis', the Rochester diocesan, Hamo de Hethe.[4] Further assistance, from the perspective of the prior and monks of Christ Church, is provided by archival material in Canterbury Cathedral Library, much of which has been made available in *Literae Cantuarienses*.[5] A number of Mepham *acta* can be painstakingly abstracted from contemporary and later registers, mainly unpublished, and from material collected by Ducarel, who incorporated extracts from the Lambeth *Registrum Album*, derived in turn from Mepham's lost register.[6]

VISITATION OF THE PROVINCE

His provincial council concluded, Mepham turned his attention to visitation, first of his diocese as we have seen, and then of the province. At the time of his provision he had secured a faculty which enabled him to visit the dioceses of his province whenever he wished. Moreover, were his visitation to be interrupted by papal or royal business he could subsequently return or progress to another diocese.[7] In the event, as has been shown in the previous chapter, he cited the monks of the cathedral priory to appear before him in the regular canonical order on the morrow of St. Gregory (13th March) 1329.

Mepham's initial provincial target was the neighbouring diocese of Rochester.[8] This followed immediately after Hethe's own visitation during which he deprived John de Frendesbury, rector of Bromley, for his obstinate rebellion, disobedience, and irrepressible malice, and collated a notable legal clerk, M. John de Penebrugg, in his place. Frendesbury arrived at Rochester cathedral on the Friday after the feast of the Holy Cross (i.e. 15 September) and with the assistance of some clerks had the presumption to excommunicate the bishop by name. At Rochester, Mepham would have reasonable expectation of Bishop Hethe's compliance or, as the author of the *Historia Roffensis* cynically observed, he could more readily overcome the poorer and less powerful.[9] Visitation, the chronicler claimed, was exercised with inhumanity and injustice; the bishop was badly treated and many expenses imposed upon him. Two contributory reasons are suggested for this, first the machinations of the accomplices of the intruder, Frendesbury, the second the odium that had arisen because Hethe had not wished to contact Masters S[imon?] and Edmund Mepham, their sisters and relatives, and to follow their advice![10]

Visitation took place on the Monday after St. Michael, 2 October 1329, when the archbishop allegedly arrived with eighty horses, and remained for a day and a night at the bishop's expense. On the morrow he visited the chapter. The total cost of visitation was £24 and no douceur was given to clerks or officers. Two casks of good ale, one pipe of wine, and ten quarters of wheat sufficed for that day. Much later, 14 November, the Tuesday after St. Martin, Mepham's clerks Masters Laurence Fastolf, Robert Brok and Robert de Weston, were sent to conduct interrogation and examination, and then to instruct the diocesan with respect to the findings brought to light by his visitation of the chapter.[11] Hethe's character, as delineated by some of the charges levelled against him,[12] was that he was quick-tempered, impatient of contradiction, someone whose word was not to be trusted—since he failed to honour his promises—and who was careless about some of his obligations as a diocesan, for instance preaching, granting of licences for non-residence, and circulating the diocese.[13] More wide ranging was the accusation that he was careless of the rights and liberties of his see and for a period of two years or thereabouts had done nothing to remedy the ravaging of his cathedral city by its citizens.[14]

There was criticism of the bishop's relationship with his cathedral priory. In the first place the process of the prior's election was flawed because, it was claimed, Hethe held the scrutiny and collation of the votes with his clerks, clandestinely and with no monk present. Consequently it was not possible for the chapter to determine on whom the 'maior pars' had determined. Although the election was declared to have been made by the 'maior et sanior pars', in fact it had been made by a very small proportion of the chapter (*a longe minori parte capituli*).[15] It lay within the bishop's authority to declare the validity of the election, and he had done so despite these irregularities. In view of such serious allegations it is surprising that no appeal was launched.

The bishop, it was claimed, had appointed twenty and more officers in the priory, rather than the regular four or five, as at Canterbury. Moreover, he had advanced his own relatives and others who did not minister in those offices but deputed others at half salary, insufficient for the carrying out of their duties. Prior to his election Hethe had promised to remedy this practice. One of his appointments was the priory's brewer who did not minister well and was of ill repute.[16] It had been an ancient custom at Rochester for the bishop on the feast of St. Andrew (30 November) to receive a gift from the chapter, estimated to be worth twenty pounds or more, in return for his obligations on that day. Hethe, however, after his creation pretended that he wished to assume the burden, received the gift, but withdrew from the obligation of undertaking the ceremony.[17] During his visitation of the monastery the bishop had admitted the denunciation of three monks of the house without proper legal process (*absque cause cognicione*) and had them deposed from their offices and imprisoned, but on hearing of Mepham's intended visitation he conceded letters of purgation to those concerned and ordered the prior to admit them.[18] Other charges also reflected the inadequacy of the bishop's pastoral activity: because of a personal dispute with William de Chelesham he had denied confirmation to his son, who then died unconfirmed; he had empowered the dean of Dartford to absolve a knight who had inflicted serious bodily harm on a priest—clearly canonically *ultra vires*; at his visitation he had failed to correct John de Woodstock, a Rochester monk accused of incontinence; he had not made sufficient provision for the burial of the parishioners at St. Nicholas, Strood, a church appropriated to the bishopric; had appointed laymen as custodians of Strood hospital, contrary to its foundation ordinance, thus leading to its ruin; and was accustomed to receive half a mark for the rendering of account of testaments (*pro reddicione raciocnii testamentorum*).[19]

Other charges were of a temporal rather than a spiritual character, such as the felling of trees, including sixty-six from Strood hospital's wood at Malling for his hall at Halling, and granting to his brother a tenement at Frekenham at a nominal rent.[20] In view of the gravity and specific nature of the charges it is surprising that Mepham, having judicially examined them and the witnesses produced, dismissed the bishop from his examination as early as 10 February 1330 on the grounds that either they could not be proved or that Hethe had advanced acceptable excuses.[21]

Roy Martin Haines

EXETER DIOCESE

After his visitation of Canterbury and Rochester dioceses Mepham, as we know incidentally from vestigial evidence, visited those of Bath and Wells, Chichester and Salisbury dioceses, according to the Rochester chronicler because of the simplicity of the bishops of those sees.[22] He was in Salisbury diocese in early August 1330 when he licensed Isabel de Cotteley to have divine service celebrated in her manor house at Cotley in Chardstock parish.[23] He held a visitation of Wells Cathedral on 16 September 1331 and celebrated the following Christmas at Wiveliscombe in Somerset.[24]

Against the advice of his council he then determined to visit Exeter. Here the archbishop was up against a determined not to say intractable upholder of the rights of his see. Bishop John Grandisson, was to hold office for 42 years—1327-1369, even longer than Hethe. He seems to have anticipated Mepham's intentions. In answer to his request John XXII issued a bull, dated 20 December 1331 from Avignon, the provisions of which were to remain in force for the duration of his episcopate. This severely curtailed the authority of the archbishop of Canterbury, his successors, and *sede vacante* that of the prior and chapter of Canterbury, whether acting by metropolitical right or by virtue of legation, visitation, or on the pretext of an appeal.[25] Disregarding this privilege Mepham cited the bishop and dean and chapter for the Monday after the Ascension 1332 (i.e. 1 June),[26] whereupon Grandisson launched an appeal. The archbishop then abandoned the order of visiting the province, not deferring to the appeal, but pressed on by every means with his visitation of the chapter. He entered the close with a few persons but found the cathedral equipped with engines of war, arms, and other military equipment, fortified just like a castle. Withdrawing under a hail of abuse, his officers having sustained many injuries, he decided that nothing would be gained from continuing what amounted to a siege. Allegedly the bishop of Exeter had the king's support.[27] There were, concluded the Rochester chronicler, many appeals to the Roman Curia on account of grievances sustained at Mepham's visitations, among them those of the bishop of Bath and Wells and of the abbot of St. Augustine's Canterbury.

THE ELA FITZPAYNE CASE

It would seem that Mepham, having visited Salisbury diocese, was in process of visiting that of Bath and Wells when he despatched a mandate to the bishop of Winchester, John Stratford, from Wiveliscombe. In its preamble he declared that like the shepherd in the Gospels he wished to find the hundredth sheep that had strayed (Luke 25.4). While in Salisbury diocese, presumably during Bishop Wyville's time,[28] he had discovered that Ela la Payne, the wife of the nobleman Robert FitzPayne, of Okeford Fitzpayne in Dorset, on account of her manifest misdoings was a lost sheep of this kind. By popular report she had committed adultery with knights and others, both single and married, and even with clerks in holy orders. Following the appropriate canonical procedures he had found Ela to be guilty, partly by reason of her confession before him, partly because of her failure to proceed successfully to purgation. He therefore decreed, in order to bring this lost sheep to the Lord's fold, that on every second and fourth day (Monday, Wednesday) of the septennium from 6 September next she was to abstain from meat, unless medical advice should dictate otherwise, in which case she should receive indulgence. Each year of the seven-year period between the festivals of St. Michael (29 September) and St. Luke the Evangelist (18 October), she was under obligation to visit the cathedral church of Salisbury, entering by the door from the cemetery adjacent to the song school. From there she was to proceed unaccompanied and barefooted from the western entry of the church to the high altar bearing a lighted wax candle four pounds in weight which she was then to offer at the altar. In pursuance of the dictum that in the same manner as water extinguishes fire, so alms extinguish sin, she was to offer 40s. to the Dominican friars, the same sum to the Franciscans, and in addition 20s. to poor persons and beggars. This was to be handed over by way of penance under the supervision of three Salisbury canons. To ensure internal humility of mind Mepham prohibited her from wearing gems and precious stones on her person or as ornaments to her saddle. She was also forbidden to paint herself as women do in red or white to make themselves more desirable to men.

To avoid occasion for delinquency by her husband due to her long absences she was required to cohabit and not to leave him save under special licence or for her journeyings to Salisbury Cathedral. In her chamber she was to have only upright company and on no account to admit John de Forde, the rector of Okeford Fitzpayne, because of their over-familiarity which has given rise to scandal. For that and other reasons she was to remove him entirely from her company. Although, declared Mepham, the penance was by no means sufficient for the enormity of her offences, he had taken account of her condition and the weakness of her sex.

The archbishop's remonstrances fell on deaf ears. It transpired that Ela Fitzpayne had not carried out her penance but continued in her evil ways. She had abstained from the customary matrimonial association with her husband, thrown aside all matronly modesty and by deed and appearance flaunted her customary insolence. For that reason he had warned certain of his suffragans in whose dioceses Ela had been in the habit of staying to warn her to perform the imposed penance within fifteen days of 17 February next, under threat of penalty and canonical censure. He had heard that she intended to stay in Winchester diocese and on his canonical obedience the diocesan was to ensure, either himself or by means of his officers, that she received a threefold warning to perform her obligations at Salisbury or to suffer excommunication. Even if she could not be apprehended in Winchester diocese the bishop was to see that these admonitions were brought to her notice, and to certify his reception of the letters about Ela and the action he had taken.

Ela Fitzpayne remained obdurate and Mepham numbered her, not among the sheep who had strayed but among those who were lost. The seventeen days having long past without response he issued another mandate on 14 April 1332 from Hinton in Dorset, within Salisbury diocese. Since she had cast aside Godly fear and all modesty, and fallen into the depths of evil, not fearing to offend the king of kings, the lord of lords, and despising the keys of the church, he had pronounced sentences of excommunication. By this means he forbade the Lord's flock, for fear of contagion, to have any contact with her. And so, Mepham reasoned, since the milk of kindness had failed to soften her the staff of the shepherd might be effective. His information was that Ela was intent on entering Winchester diocese at Southwark, Rotherhithe and elsewhere, staying for some days, and mixing with the faithful. Bishop Stratford, he declared, was under obligation to assist him in maintaining ecclesiastical discipline throughout his diocese and to publicise the sentences in his cathedral and every other church in the city and diocese—especially Southwark and Rotherhithe. Rectors vicars and parish priests were to make public declaration of the excommunication on Sundays and feast days during the solemnities of the Mass with bells ringing, candles lit and then extinguished—a potent symbol of perdition. This was to be done under threat of compulsion should they prove negligent. Furthermore, enquiry was to be undertaken by the diocesan Official and other trustworthy subjects as to the names of those unlawfully contacting the excommunicate: guilty parties were to be cited before the archbishop wherever he might be in the province. Mepham also revealed, and this doubtless prompted the mandate to Stratford, that new findings about Ela had been discovered during his visitation of Bath and Wells.[29]

At this point, so far as the Winchester register is concerned, Ela Payne or Fitzpayne fades into obscurity, although the Rochester chronicler notes that Ela appealed as a consequence of the archbishop's action during his visitation of Salisbury and Chichester.[30] We do not learn of the action taken by Bishop Stratford in response to Mepham's mandates. His register does contain a quire of legal processes but this does not include cases beyond the early part of 1329. The bishop was to be translated to Canterbury in November of 1333 when he was succeeded at Winchester by the former bishop of Worcester, Adam Orleton. The case provides an indication of the difficulty the church encountered in disciplining recalcitrant nobility whose means enabled them to move easily from one jurisdiction to another, and could on occasion evade ecclesiastical censure.

THE NORWICH 'SEDE VACANTE' COMPOSITION

Sede vacante compositions resulted from conflicts between archbishops and the cathedral chapters of suffragan sees deprived of their incumbents. Those for London, Salisbury, Worcester,[31] and Norwich are printed in Dr. Churchill's, *Canterbury Administration*.[32] All save the last date from the time of Archbishop Boniface (1245-70). At Norwich Archbishop Reynolds's visitation during the vacancy following Bishop Salmon's death in 1325 was claimed to be an encroachment on the chapter's rights and appeal was made to the Apostolic See. It was against this background that Mepham negotiated the composition which, as Prior Eastry remarked, was safer than having interminable suits *(lites quasi immortales)* in the Roman Curia.[33] A caution which the archbishop was to overlook when it came to his conflict with St. Augustine's.

The agreement enshrined in the composition of August 1330[34] between Bishop William Airmynne or Airmyn of Norwich, Prior William de Claxton, his chapter, and Archbishop Mepham, was to the following effect. Whenever the see of Norwich fell vacant in the future the archbishop at the time would be entitled to exercise for the whole of the vacancy the same jurisdiction as did the bishop *sede plena*, except for visitation of the chapter, city and diocese, and enquiry into, correction and punishment of crimes, defects and excesses arising from the findings. But within fifteen days of any vacancy the chapter was to present three names to the archbishop, his Official, or other representative, so that he could choose one for the purpose of such visitation and correction. The operation of this composition is first clearly to be seen following the death Bishop Bateman in January 1355, the relevant documents having been printed by Dr. Churchill from Archbishop Islep's register.[35]

Endnotes

1. McHardy, 'The Loss of Archbishop Stratford's Register'.
2. *Chronica Thorne* and *Historia Roffensis*. For the authorship of the latter and the relationship between H. Wharton's text in *Anglia Sacra* and the MS. see Haines, 'Bishops and Politics in the Reign of Edward II', pp. 590-1, and for other facets of Hethe's episcopate, idem, 'The Episcopate of a Benedictine monk: Hamo de Hethe', pp. 102-207. Buck in the *ODNB* s.v. 'Hythe' only goes so far as to suggest that the *Historia* was 'written by a clerk in his [the bishop's] entourage'. Much detail can of course be gleaned from *Rochester Reg. Hethe*.
3. HR, fo. 51^v: 'modum et mores hominum totaliter ignorans'.
4. *Thorne* is in Twysden ed., *Historiae Anglicana*; Spelman, *Concilia, Decreta, Leges* (London 1664) ii, and for a partial version of Dene's 'Historia Roffensis' [see n.2 above], Wharton, *Anglia Sacra*. Unfortunately the register of the contemporary dean of the province, Bishop Stephen Gravesend (1318-38), is rudimentary. See *Registrum Radulphi Baldock etc.*
5. There are also unpublished act books of the early phase of the pontificate and of the years 1328-30 in the archives of the Dean and Chapter of Canterbury: Dcc ChAnt/A/36/i-ii. See Appendix 5 below.
6. See Appendix 1 below and BL. Add. MS. 6066, Ducarel, *Fragmenta*. Ducarel's extracts come principally from the Lambeth Registrum Album, DCc Reg. Q (which he terms 'P') and from such printed sources as Wilkins, *Concilia*, and Spelman, *Concilia, Decreta, Leges*.
7. CCA DCc Reg. I, fos. 427^v-8^r, Avignon 14 July 1328. See above, p. 37 n. 39. It was regular practice for archbishops and bishops at the time of their promotion at the Curia to secure benefits of this or other kinds. Reynolds had certainly done so. He was permitted to make visitation without observing the order established by Pope Innocent IV. Wright, *Reynolds*, pp. 59-62; HMC 9th Rep., p. 74a.
8. The account in HR, fos. 53^{r-v}, is in two parts separated by details of Hethe's own troubled visitation of his diocese.

9   Ibid., fo. 53ʳ. 'Archiepiscopo tunc consilio suo vocato disposuit provinciam visitare, et agressus est primo pauperiorem et impotenciorem invadere episcopum Roffensem quia eum facilius potuit superare'.

10   Ibid. fo. 53ᵛ. 'Procurantibus complicibus illius intrusoris archiepiscopo assistentibus, ac eciam ex causa odii et invidie inveterate quia episcopus Magistros S. et E. de Mepham et eorum sorores et parentes ad se vocare noluit et consilium eorum sequi'. Is the 'S' an error or was there another Mepham possibly also named Simon?

11   HR, fo. 53v. 'ad interogandum, examinandum et requirendum episcopum super compertis et delatis per capitulum Roffensem in visitacione sua.' The more usual word found in conjunction with 'comperta' is 'detecta'. *Worc. Admin.*, p. 151.

12   There are 25 charges which in the following footnotes are numbered 1-25. They are enumerated in the editor's résumé which prefaces the document of 10 February 1330 detailing them. *Rochester Reg. Hethe*, pp. 424-8.

13   *Rochester Reg. Hethe*, nos. 11: 'episcopus est impaciens et de facili escandescit in homines quando aliquid dicitur contra voluntatem suam'; 12: 'est inconstans in dictis, promissa non adimplens'; 6: 'raro predicat in dyocesi sua'; 1: 'literas vagas dispensacionis per unum annum continuum ab ecclesia tua pro negociis tuis te absentare valeas'; 4: 'non circuit dyocesim ut tenetur pro officio episcopali impenddendo (*sic*), set moratur apud Halling' et Trottesc[liffe], et licet alquando transeat per Waldas [Weald], non confirmat pueros, de quo magnum murmur est'.

14   No. 2. Of course this fails to take account of the disturbed state of the country as a whole.

15   No. 9. 'Pronunciat sic dicendo, 'Quia talem invenimus a majori et saniori parte capituli electum, ipsum preficimus in priorem', licet a longe minori parte capituli forsan fuisset electum'. John of Westerham was elected prior 14 Jan. 1320, but died early the following year. This refers to his successor John of Speldhurst elected 31 Jan. 1321, resigned 19 August 1333. At Mepham's visitation he was said to be illegitimate and Bishop Hethe was accused of having ignored the fact. No. 8; *BRECP*, pp. 638-9; *Heads of Religious Houses*, p. 62.

16   Nos. 16-18.

17 No. 19.

18 No. 13. The three monks concerned were Henry de Henxeye, Robert de Morton, and John de Oxonia. They had appealed to the archbishop. *BRECP*, pp. 610 (*s.v.* Hengseye), 623, 625.

19 Nos. 5, 7, 10, 21, 22, 25.

20 Nos. 24, 20, also 3, 14, 23.

21 *Rochester Reg. Hethe*, p. 428. 'Consideratis deposicionibus testium productorum ac aliis adminiculis que pro dicto domino episcopo faciunt in hac parte, ipsum dominum episcopum super omnibus criminibus, excessibus, et defectibus predictis... sentencialiter et diffinitive dimittimus per presentes'.

22 HR, fo. 60^v: 'per simplicitatem episcoporum diocesium predictarum'. The 'simple' bishops were Ralph of Shrewsbury, John Langton, and Robert Wyville.

23 Cornwall Record Office bAR/1/1029. The licence is dated 7 August.

24 See Appendix 1.

25 *Exeter Reg. Grandisson*, p. 138. 'Fraternitati tue ut quamdiu ecclesie Exoniensi prefueris, tu, aut officiales tui cujuscumque status et condicionis existant, a venerabili fratre nostro archiepiscopo Cantuariensi metropolitano tuo, vel successoribus suis, archiepiscopis Cantuariensibus qui pro tempore fuerint, seu officialibus eorundem, aut a dilectis filiis, priore et capitulo ecclesie Cantuariensis, sive quovis alio iurisdiccionem quamlibet, dicta ecclesia Cantuariensi vacante, in provincia Cantuariensi de jure vel consuetudine excercente, jure metropolitico, seu legationis vel visitacionis aut appellationis pretextu, aliave occasione seu causa quacumque, excommunicari aut suspendi, vel tu, aut dicta ecclesia Exoniensis, seu capelle tue, interdici minime valeatis, vel tua, seu tuorum officialium prefatorum bona, in quibusvis ipsius partibus existencia, sequestrari non possint, auctoritate presencium indulgemus...'

26 This date is supplied by Baker, *Chronicon*, p. 50 and *Murimuth*, p. 65, where at n. 8 is an extract on the same matter and under the same date from BL Harl. MS. 1729.

27 HR, fos. 60^v-61^r. '... quia archiepiscopus pretermisso ordine visitandi provinciam Cant' visitare inchoavit. Archiepiscopo tunc appellacionem non defferente satagebat modis omnibus saltim capitulum visitare, clausum ecclesie cathedralis cum paucis

intrans, ecclesiam cathedralem machinis armis et alio apparatu ad bellum sicuti castrum munitam [um?] invenit. Recedens illius conviciis et contumeliis ipse et omnes sui affecti iniuriis multis lassessiti ministri eius et familiares vulnerati; Exon' episcopo regali potestate favente'.

28 Bishop Martival's register has been published by the Canterbury and York Society, but he died in 14 Mar. 1330. That of his successor, Robert Wyville (1330-75), is now housed in the Wiltshire and Swindon History Centre at Chippenham, D1/2/3-

29 Winchester Reg. Stratford, fos. 70^r-71^r; edn. nos. 682-3.

30 HR, fo. 61^r.

31 See Haines, 'The Administration of the diocese of Worcester *Sede vacante*, 1266-1350', pp. 156-71.

32 *Canterbury Administration*, ii. pp. 41-79.

33 *Lit. Cant.* 1, p. 517.

34 The document was sealed by the prior and chapter 4 August 1330 at Norwich, and by Bishop Airmynne (Airmyn) at Canterbury on 6 August. Possibly the latter date was also that of Mepham's sealing. *Canterbury Administration*, I, pp. 196-7; ii. pp. 64-9, where the composition is printed in full. CCA ChAnt/N/4-

35 Ibid, pp. 70-4. Early in 1355 Archbishop Islep issued commissions to an Official *sede vacante*, a corrector and sequestrator, and others for visitation of the priory and the city and diocese, in response to the request of the prior and chapter in accordance with the composition.

Chapter Five

PROVINCIAL COUNCILS AND CONVOCATIONS

THE PROVINCIAL COUNCIL OF 1329

According to Prior Eastry Pope John XXII had repeatedly encouraged (*crebris monitis excitati*) Mepham to hold a provincial council as soon as possible.[1] Ideally such councils ought to have been held annually: 'On the authority of the Holy Fathers the Digest decreed that in all provinces once a year general councils should be celebrated so that evil doings might be corrected and diligent discussion held about excesses, especially those of the clergy.'[2] They almost never were, and in any case it is sometimes difficult to distinguish between such councils and convocations.[3] It would seem that Reynolds did not hold one *eo nomine*. Stratford was to hold three: in 1341, 1342 and 1347.[4] Mepham responded to the pope's suggestion prior to the end of the first year from his consecration. The council was to be held on the Friday after the Conversion of St. Paul, 27 January 1329.

Before they directed their steps towards London and the council the bishops were ordered to deliberate with their clergy and to enquire sagaciously about grievances and defects requiring reformation. In addition they were to see that clergy and people held processions, litanies and other prayers for the peace of the realm and for the success of the council. At Winchester Stratford did not conduct these enquiries in person because, as we have seen, political activity prevented his so doing. Instead, by mandates dated 23 December 1328 from Southwark, he instructed the archdeacons of Winchester and Surrey, or their officials, to implement the archbishop's mandate.[5] Unfortunately his episcopal register does not record the result of their deliberations. Prior Eastry, was likewise unable to attend, doubtless because of the state of his health at the time, but he duly appointed proctors.[6]

Much is known about Bishop Grandisson's response with regard to Exeter diocese. His certificate is dated 18 January from Chudleigh in Devon and enumerates those cited: the dean of the cathedral, seven abbots, eleven priors, the archdeacons of Exeter, Barnstaple, Totnes and Cornwall, the cathedral chapter and the colleges of Holy Cross, Crediton; St. Thomas the Martyr, Glasney; and Crantock. His excuses were detailed in a lengthy letter to the archbishop dated the following day. In it, among other impediments, he urged the hazards likely to be encountered in a volatile London. In his own case the venue was particularly dangerous in that the pope had promised to arrange an enquiry into the death of his predecessor, Walter Stapeldon, and rumour had it that he was commissioned for that purpose. Moreover, the interior of his London house had been gutted and its contents carried off. He despatched another letter to bishops Stratford of Winchester, Orleton of Worcester, and Gravesend of London, in the hope that they would support his position and doubtless look favourably on the *gravamina* he was submitting.[7] These *gravamina* are itemised as follows: firstly, lay lords did not permit their villeins (*nativi et servi*) to make wills; secondly, secular judges in the diocese usurped cognisance in purely spiritual suits and, worse still, by secular power dragged ecclesiastics into causes which by reason of the persons and the matters involved pertained to the ecclesiastical forum; and finally, although the remedy of appeal was established, not to defend iniquity but as a safeguard for the innocent, certain incorrigible subjects have appealed from lawful and canonical correction to the Court of Canterbury and from the presidents of that court have too easily obtained inhibitions, thus eluding ecclesiastical correction and persevering in their evil ways and rebelliousness.[8]

Most of the chroniclers, not surprisingly the *Annales Paulini* is an exception, throw little light on the proceedings. Dene is dismissive: nothing was done it was a costly affair and grievances were not addressed, the participants left empty-handed in more ways than one. The bishop of Rochester, Hamo de Hethe, who never ceased to emphasise the poverty of his see, seems to have been disillusioned: he retired to his manor of Halling where he spent the whole of the following Lent and Summer.[9] Baker, who follows Murimuth closely at this point, considered that something of weight had been achieved and enumerates the regulations for the observance of Good Friday and All Souls without any servile labour, and the prayers on the feast of the Conception of the Virgin for God's absolution. The archbishop, he says, joined all the suffragan bishops in pronouncing sentence of excommunication against the murderers outside St. Paul's on 15 October 1326, of Walter Stapeldon, bishop of Exeter, and their aiders and abettors.[10]

Elements of the proceedings can be pieced together from various sources. Mass of the Holy Spirit was celebrated by John Langton, the bishop of Chichester. This was accompanied by singing of the *Veni Creator Spiritus*. Mepham preached a sermon *ad clerum*—that is in Latin. On the final day, 10 February, the bishop of Norwich, William Ayrminne or Airmyn, celebrated a mass for peace. The sentences of excommunication followed the gospel and besides Stapeldon's murderers included those who had ransacked the abbeys of Bury St. Edmund's and Abingdon.[11] This was clearly intended to bring to a close the factional disputes of the previous reign which had served to generate the violent behaviour of the Londoners. What the chroniclers do not dwell upon are the abuses which the constitutions sought to redress or the manner of their publication in the dioceses.

Endnotes

1. *Lit. Cant.*, i. no. 266.
2. Winchester Reg. Stratford, fo. 72ᵛ, edn. no. 694. *Extra* 5, 1, 25 *Sicut olim*, from Lateran IV, c. 6.
3. Wright, *Reynolds*, p. 76 n. 30, certainly thought so.
4. *Abp. Stratford*, App. 3.
5. *Win.RS*, fo. 43ʳ, edn. no. 441; *Records of Convocation III*, pp. 109-10.
6. *Lit. Cant.*, i. nos 266-8. He had hoped to attend the council but added a caveat: 'juxta mei corporis qualitatem'.
7. *Records of Convocation III*, pp. 105-8, where the relevant documents, including the archbishop's mandate, are printed from Grandisson's MS register.
8. Ibid., p. 105.
9. *Ann. Paulini*, p. 344; HR, fo. 52ᵛ. 'In concilio antedicto nulla fuerunt expedita sed sicuti prelati et clerus in magnis sumptibus ad concilium venerunt ita vacui sine reparacione gravaminum ecclesie recesserunt.'
10. Baker, *Chronicon*, p. 43; *Murimuth*, p. 59: 'ordinavit aliqua, licet modicum ponderanda . . . Item archiepiscopus statuit, de consensu concilii, quod festum Conceptionis beatae Mariae solempnitur celebratur; et quaedam alia'.
11. *Ann. Paulini*, pp. 344-5. Details of the excommunications are in the *Annales Paulini* and in Lambeth MS. 1106, fo. 106 (the relevant extract is in *Exeter Reg. Grandisson*, p. 1539). For Bury see Lobel, 'The rising at Bury St. Edmund's'.

Chapter Six

THE FATAL STRUGGLE WITH ST. AUGUSTINE'S, CANTERBURY

ATTEMPTED VISITATION: ARCHIEPISCOPAL CITATION

While engaged in Canterbury Mepham also visited St. Augustine's abbey. The evidence for his actions and those of his legal antagonist, the abbey, is provided voluminously by Thorne's chronicle on the one hand and by the *Literae Cantuarienses* on the other. Thorne provides transcripts or partial transcripts of many documents, but seldom dates them. The Canterbury documents are regularly dated. Unfortunately, although the basic aspects of the controversy are clear enough in both cases, and are broadly in agreement, there are considerable divergences of detail and sometimes of fact.

In Thorne's view the archbishop treated the abbey extremely roughly (*graviter molestavit et multipliciter perturbavit*). He is said to have summoned Abbot Ralph de Borne[1] and the convent to appear before him and the auditors of his court at irregular places (*loca incerta*), with a demand to view their privileges, rights, and the appropriation documents of their churches: St. Paul's Canterbury, Sturry, Faversham, Preston,[2] Milton, Minster with its chapels,

Lenham, Tenterden, Kennington, Northbourne with its chapels, and Chislet—all in Kent.[3] The undated text of his summons is given in full by Thorne. On the grounds that they ought not to appear, the monks did not respond. They were declared contumacious, the archbishop reserving the penalty to himself. Having endured all these injuries and vexations, as they considered them, the monks appealed to the apostolic see for a remedy. Thereupon Pope John XXII issued a bull, dated 22 July 1330,[4] to Itherius or Itier de Concoreto, a canon of Salisbury, detailing St. Augustine's claim that since its foundation and beyond the memory of man it had enjoyed exemption by special papal privilege from the jurisdiction of the Ordinary. A privilege of Boniface VIII had further conceded that this extended not only to the abbey but also to all its 'members', churches, chapels, and subjects. The judge then sentenced Mepham to pay £700 to the abbey to levy which Itherius on apostolic authority imposed sequestration on the archbishop's goods.

In fact Pope Boniface had issued two bulls, dated respectively 27 February 1300 (*Circumspecta*) and 19 March (*Dudum*) of the same year, both from the Lateran. The first contains a very full exposition of the abbey's exemption from any exercise of diocesan or metropolitan authority—by the Ordinary, the archbishop of Canterbury, or the prior and convent *sede vacante*, whether on the grounds of delegation, tuition or under any other pretence. The second bull reinforces these privileges and specifically denounces action taken subsequently by Archbishop Winchelsey.[5] Regardless of these exemptions, and despite being given full and sufficient notice of them, Archbishop Simon was alleged to have troubled the abbey, its churches and people, with various nuisances, issuing citations and warning them of impending visitation. The pope therefore inhibited Mepham meanwhile from doing anything to the abbey's prejudice. The abbey's muniments were duly exhibited to Itherius de Concoreto on the eve of St. Michael (i.e. 28 September 1330). In obedience to them Concoreto, as judge, was urged to proceed in the matter and order the archbishop's citation. This he did in obedience to the apostolic mandates.[6]

PLUMSTEAD CHURCH, KENT

Much later in the chronicle, somewhat out of sequence, Thorne gives an account of the archbishop's visitation of Plumstead, a church in Rochester diocese appropriated to St. Augustine's. The religious had received many citations and subsequent sentences respecting the appropriation which, as was their right by reason of their exemption, they had not appeared to answer. Mepham, therefore, excommunicated the chaplains of the church and of the chapel of East Wickham, as well as the parishioners, although allegedly they had not been lawfully cited, condemned, or contumaciously absent, so that all rule of law had been disregarded. The archbishop ordered the rural dean of Dartford to publish their excommunication and that of all who communicated with them. In addition the dean was to cite them to give reason why their caption and incarceration should not be sought from the king's majesty.

About the same time the archbishop's commissaries and auditors of causes sitting judicially in the church of Erith forewarned the priests and people, whereupon M. Laurence de Yford, proctor of the abbot, cautioned that these were connected to the abbey as they had confirmed that very morning in the presence of a notary. They expressly wished to maintain their provocations and appeals, one of them declaring that in this they did well. Immediately the archbishop's chancellor excommunicated priests and parishioners in writing and assigned a day for the abbey's proctor, M. Walter Pycard, to respond to the findings made at the visitation. At that point question was made as to the nature of these findings, to which the reply was that this would transpire later. Not content with this, grievance was piled upon grievance by the removal from office and suspension of the advocates and notaries acting for the abbot's defence. Appeal was then made on behalf of the church of Plumstead, requesting that the archbishop and his commissaries be inhibited from prejudicing the abbey's jurisdiction or judging the case.

The benefice's legal position, comprising six points, was placed before Itherius, in his capacity as judge. Firstly, Plumstead had long belonged to the abbey. Secondly, both church and people were and had been exempt by the authority of the apostolic see from any jurisdiction of or subjection to the archbishop of Canterbury or the bishop of Rochester, their officials or commissaries, but were lawfully subject to the abbey. Thirdly, the abbot in person or through his commissaries had been exercising jurisdiction in the church in the full knowledge of archbishops and bishops without any contradiction, wholly, peacefully, and without cessation. Fourthly, the present abbot, for the whole of his time has been in possession of the exercise of the said jurisdiction among clerks and laymen celebrating in the church and staying there. Fifthly, all these things were public and known throughout the dioceses of Canterbury and Rochester and in neighbouring areas. Lastly, all the above claims were verified by various attestations.

The judge then ordered the production of witnesses wishing to testify to the abbey's exemption and to ensure its perpetual memory. For this purpose were produced the monks Thomas Poucy D.Th., Richard de Canterbury, Thomas de Natyndon, Thomas Wyvelesberg, and Thomas Colwell, Masters John de Schorditch,[7] Laurence Yford, John de Grove, and others, archdeacons, rectors and vicars, as well as seculars, about a hundred in number. The archbishop having received their attestations, although called to judgement very many times, did not appear either in person or by a proctor. At length on behalf of the abbey M. Walter Pycard appeared before Itherius in his London house, where he was interrogated on oath about the expenditure occurred by the chaplains and parishioners. He replied that it amounted to two hundred marks and more, whereupon the judge condemned Mepham to pay that sum as damages arising from his actions.[8]

THE STRUGGLE WITH THE PAPAL NUNCIO

Why Mepham, in defiance of the abbey's clearly defined exemption, chose to blunder into what turned out to be a hornet's nest is difficult to comprehend. It may be that his earlier petition of 14 July 1328, before returning from the Roman Curia, and mentioned above in chapter 2, was intended to provide room for unfettered action, but in any case he could scarcely have hoped to ride roughshod over well-established jurisdictional exemptions from metropolitan authority. Inevitably his actions precipitated a hazardous train of events leading to expensive litigation, contumacy, and inevitable condemnation. According to Thorne's account, which seems to have been confirmed by subsequent events, the archbishop used every means to evade Itherius's jurisdiction, and in response to Aymericus, rector of St. Julian, his proctor for citation, questioned his objectivity as a judge by claiming that the nuncio was a yearly pensioner of the abbey and its special counsellor, hence too favourably inclined towards its interests.[9] The monks alleged further that the archbishop claimed to have been put in personal jeopardy (*sub poena capitis sui*) by Itherius who had cited him to a remote place, which could only be reached by dangerous and insecure ways inappropriate to his status. For these and other deceitful reasons the archbishop was said to have asked the pope for other arbitrators, whereupon the abbey's proctor was sent to the Roman Court bearing a document elaborating their grievances.

The abbey's proctor then submitted the monks' interpretation of the matter. The archbishop, in contempt of the pope and the apostolic see had 'bulled' (*inbullavit*) the papal delegate before the king, earls, barons and prelates in parliament, apparently that meeting at Westminster in September 1331,[10] whither he had cited M. Itherius de Concoreto to respond to certain articles which pertained to the crown and not to the ecclesiastical forum. By this course of action, Mepham is said to have argued, the nuncio became guilty of *lèse majesté*, should be punished, and prohibited by royal letters from proceeding against him. Thereupon, incited by the archbishop, certain nobles called for Itherius to be removed from the realm. But there was such a clamour by the bishops of Winchester, John Stratford, and Worcester, Adam Orleton, among other prelates, that maturer counsel prevailed. Instead, Itherius was summoned for the following day to reply to the archbishop.

The nuncio's response was devastating. He, Itherius, had not cited the archbishop in parliament, nor had him cited, but in Chichester diocese by the diocesan bishop,

John Langton, whose certificatory letter he produced. He had not made any citation concerning articles affecting the royal crown, but because of Mepham's violation of an oath of fealty taken to the pope, and for many other reasons. The king could not and ought not to proceed to a prohibition in such matters, because the king was neither the author of the canons nor their corrector.[11] All these things, he declared, the archbishop had done in contempt of his holiness, the pope, and to the severe injury and prejudice of his monastery. He declared them to be notorious and the archbishop thereby publicly diffamed. It was not true, the proctor added, that Mepham had been cited to an obscure location, but to London, a notable place, in which the archbishop had his metropolitan court and near the centre of which Itherius occupied one of the greater houses. As to the allegation that Itherius's position was suspect, that was false, for it should not be thought that a servant of the apostolic see could be a pensioner or clerk of anyone. All the above, he concluded, were designed to frustrate the process; he therefore sought remedy on behalf of the abbey and requested that the pope punish and correct the archbishop and other culpable persons as an example. And so, Thorne continues, the pope having learned and pondered Mepham's subterfuges, and being adequately informed by the proctors of Itherius and those of the abbey, ordered his delegate to pursue the case.

THE SLINDON FRACAS

Significantly perhaps, it was on the feast of St. Benedict, 21 March 1331, that Br. Thomas de Natyndon, a monk of St. Augustine's acting as proctor of the abbot and convent, Aymericus de Rogesio, and Thomas Mancel, a notary public, together with others, proceeded on Itherius's order to the archbishop's manor of Slindon in Sussex. This lay in Chichester diocese where Mepham may recently have been conducting a visitation. They attempted to cite the archbishop and entered the hall of the manor. Thereupon some fifty men of the archbishop's household rushed upon them with swords and cudgels, heavily beat Aymericus and cheerfully inflicted blows on his body. Not content with that they caught and stripped him.

Thus nude, with his hands tied behind his back and his feet tethered, he was thrust into prison. So tightened by a stick was the cord that he nearly expired. His head was scraped so that he would not appear a priest, and thus incarcerated almost six gallons of freezing water were thrown on him and he was held in this torment for at least one night. These rioters broke Thomas Mancel's arm in two places and beat him grievously. Br. Thomas Natyndon, feeling that he was in danger of death, fled in terror. He was pursued tumultuously to Henry Percy's manor of Petworth where he was imprisoned for three days. At length he escaped from their hands in the name of God. On the morrow of the feast of the Invention of the Holy Cross, that is 4 May (1331?), what had happened at Slindon was laid before the pope and cardinals in consistory by the abbey's advocate. The pope is said to have been angry and, shaking his head, to have declared that he was under obligation to administer equal justice. In this case because the fact was so notorious purgation should not be denied, but in the circumstances purgation would be worthless, so that condign punishment for these faults should fall on Mepham's head.

Already the archbishop had made his response. Adopting a detached stance, he alleged in a sworn deposition that his chancellor had recently told him that a certain Br. Thomas de Natyndon with his accomplices, whose names were unknown to him, with arms that were both defensive and offensive, entered his manor of Slindon without permission from the gatekeeper. He was himself in his chamber afflicted with a severe illness so that the monk was told he could not speak with the archbishop on this occasion because of his illness. Irritated by this rebuff the monk and his accomplices exchanged insults with certain of the archbishop's familiars. At length two of the said accomplices were wounded and even arrested outside the manor gate and at and after clamorous pursuit by various persons, whose names are likewise unknown, this monk was captured and arrested within Henry de Percy's liberty of at Petworth. On the Holy Gospels Mepham swore that he had not approved any of this, but detested it.

It was true, continued Thorne, that the archbishop had permanently removed those culpable from his house and *familia*. This he had done so that that he could appear an innocent before Itherius, and to restore his reputation (*bona fama*) which had been besmirched in both the Roman Curia and in England. In an attempt to remove the slur on his reputation Mepham's proctor sought to establish proof that his good character had been acknowledged, both in the city and in the dioceses of London, Chichester, Lincoln, York, and throughout the province of Canterbury, in the realm of England and the Roman Curia, over ten, twenty and thirty years, both near and far (*citra & ultra*), as an upright man of honest conversation, co-operative, modest, gentle, humble and kind-hearted, and as such reputed throughout the English realm. As proof the bishops of London (Gravesend), Lincoln (Burghersh), Worcester (Orleton), Carlisle (Ross), Norwich (Ayrminne), Chichester (John Langton), Salisbury (Wyville) and Ely (Hothum), lent their names to letters patent drawn up by the bishop of London, the dean of the province.[12] In addition the archbishop produced regular clergy and laymen (*fratres et laici seculares*), thirty-two in number, to testify to his good fame and the fact that he had not provided counsel or help (*consilium vel favorem*) in the Slindon affair. But, comments Thorne, they did so out of fear of the archbishop and his disapproval, not daring to do otherwise. Thus either knowingly or unknowingly they committed perjury.

The monks had then to put their case. The archbishop of Aix-en-Provence, Armand de Narcès, had been commissioned by the pope to carry out an investigation. Having done so, he submitted his findings. Not surprisingly his version of events, abstracted from the monks and their supporters, completely contradicted that circulated on Mepham's behalf. Clearly either the archbishop or his officers had been responsible for the enormities. He must surely have heard or even seen something but did nothing to stop the fracas, although this would have been easy and his word alone would have sufficed. This flew in contempt of the pope and the apostolic see, as well as being to the abbey's substantial injury. Twenty-four witnesses were produced, but had the case been concluded in England the archbishop's number could have been tripled.[13] All were diligently examined on oath one-by-one on the matter of the archbishop's notorious ill-fame in the neighbourhood of Slindon. Public opinion, they claimed, was that he ordered the excesses and that at the time both knew they were being committed and heard them taking place. Had he wished he could easily have put a stop to them. They occurred outside the chamber where he was at the time and for this he is notoriously defamed among clerks and laymen throughout the realm of England. The witnesses also said that Br. Thomas Natyndon, the abbey's proctor, read the citation in the hall of the manor and a squire came and asked him what he was doing, to which he responded that he was doing what was incumbent on him by ecclesiastical law. The squire replied that he feared he would die. Natyndon's response was that even if he did he was carrying out the church's laws. The witnesses added that it had been the squire who had ordered the commission of the atrocities, so that when other bishops duly declared the perpetrators excommunicate, Mepham did not wish to denounce any one of them.

Meanwhile Register L, a Canterbury letter-book, reveals that in about April (1332?) the prior of Christ Church Canterbury had received from the archbishop's commissary certain letters patent relevant to the suit, which he had caused to be published in Christ Church and in the church of St. Augustine, in the presence of notaries and others. With the assent of the commissary he proposed to retain the originals so that, among other things, the monks of St. Augustine's could make a copy. He added that from an agent at the Curia he had learned that on 4 May the pope in Consistory had ordered the monks to exhibit their original exemption, about which the archbishop might wish to write to him (*vos ut credo non latente, dignemini plenius scribere michi*).[14] This co-operative attitude towards St. Augustine's is also reflected in a cordial letter to the abbot carried by Br. W. de Coventre one of the monks from the priory, probably in July of the same year.[15]

On his way to the Curia in July 1332 the archbishop's messenger John de Cornubia was taken ill at Beauvais and, because his life was despaired of, Thomas de Wouhope was sent after him to collect the papers he was carrying. While proceedings were taking place at Avignon, Itherius continued his process against Mepham in England. By means of a representative (*minister*), accompanied by a notary, he sent him details of all the injustices which the archbishop had wrongly inflicted on the abbey, to which he demanded an immediate response under penalty of the law, to be brought back by the bearer. On receipt of this denunciation Mepham did not respond in person but put words into the mouth of an official, who declared that his archbishop did not accept Itherius as a judge in the case because he had appealed against him (*ab ipso appellavit*) and therefore was not under obligation to reply to the arguments presented, but from a grievance (*ab gravamine*), if that were necessary within the time permitted by law.

CONDEMNATION AND EXCOMMUNICATION

On receipt of this reply Itherius, entitled papal nuncio in England, Scotland, Wales and Ireland, and sole judge in the case of the appeal of the religious of St. Augustine's abbey, their subjects, and the parishioners of their churches, ordered Bishop John Langton, the abbot of Waltham—Richard of Hertford (1308-45), the prior of Lewes—John de Courtenay,[16] and Aymer de Rogesio, rector of St. Julian, to have the archbishop cited. Under threat of excommunication for disobedience they, or any one or two of them, as should be required, were to execute the mandate without delay. In the event of their being able to approach the archbishop in safety he was to be cited, and told that whether he came or not he would be proceeded against, notwithstanding his absence or contumacy.

The abbey's proctors put in an appearance before Itherius, charged the archbishop with contumacy, and asked the judge to make pronouncement to that effect and to declare him obstructive.[17] They suggested that the judge should direct summonses and other judicial mandates to his metropolitan church for execution since anyone sent on their behalf would not dare to approach the archbishop for fear of death. In addition they sought to be absolved *ad cautelam* from the sentence of excommunication passed against them on account of their appeal and contumacy. Because, Thorne continues, the judge considered the abbey's appeal to have a ring of truth, by his subsequent acts and on the authority of his jurisdiction, he approved it. In consequence Br. Stephen de Hakendon appeared in the London house of the judge and sought declaration of the archbishop as contumacious, he not having appeared to answer any citation, and the assignment of a day for hearing definitive sentence. This the judge accepted and ordered Mepham's conviction for 'malice' to be pronounced throughout Canterbury deanery, as well as his citation to hear definitive sentence and to give reason why he should not be condemned to pay lawful damages and expenses to the religious. There being no response to the citation by the archbishop or anyone on his behalf Itherius proceeded to definitive sentence. This is undated but is thoroughgoing. The abbey's exemptions were clear and well substantiated, Mepham had knowledge of them but proceeded nonetheless. All his actions and those of his officers concerning the abbey and its possessions were therefore unlawful, injurious and unjust. He was condemned to pay expenses which had still to be assessed.

DAMAGES, DEPRESSION, AND DEATH

According to documents from Canterbury Letter Book L printed in *Literae Cantuarienses*, which are not matched in the material provided by Thorne, Itherius de Concoreto issued a directive collectively to the bishops of Worcester (Orleton), Exeter (Grandisson), and Bath and Wells (Ralph of Shrewsbury), the abbot of Langdon, the priors of Horton and Bermondsey, the archdeacon of Lewes, M. William de Nassyngton, Bernard Viventius, canon of St. Emilion, Bordeaux, the official of the archdeacon of Canterbury, and the rural deans of Westbere, Sandwich, Bridge, Lympne, and Charing. This contains a recension of the bull of 22 July 1330 condemning the archbishop's interference with the abbey's exempt jurisdiction, and requires the commissaries under penalty of excommunication to secure the sequestration of the archbishop's goods up to the sum of £700 as costs.[18] He continued his process in the cathedral church of Canterbury on 22 January 1333 by declaring that if Mepham did not pay the £700 within thirty days he would be *ipso facto* suspended from holding divine services. Were he to remain obdurate for a further period of thirty days he would be excommunicated.[19]

The archbishop died in a state of excommunication on 12 October 1333, a fact which Thorne does not record at this point. Instead, according to the printed edition, it was on 1 December (presumably 1332) that Itherius ordered the prior of the Augustinian house of St. Gregory, Canterbury,[20] to cite the archbishop in his cathedral of Christ Church, Canterbury, to appear on the day following the feast of St. Lucy (13 December), unless a feast day, otherwise the next appropriate day thereafter, in the judge's London house, to hear the amount of his taxation. This would be determined whether Mepham came or not. The proctor of St. Augustine's estimated that throughout the suit necessary expenses amounted to £1,210 or more, not counting the maintenance of clerks, which was left for the judge's decision. This sum was sworn to by one Godfrey or Geoffrey[21] Barown, a clerk aged twenty-four who declared that in the following March it would be three years since the monks had appealed to the apostolic see. Various men, notably lawyers had acted in the Roman court and in England as proctors, advocates, counsellors, notaries public, scriptors, promoters and witnesses. There were also messengers going to and returning from the Curia, remaining there, as well as other people labouring in the case. Then there was the necessary food and drink. When asked how he knew that so much money had been spent he replied that he saw, heard, was personally present, and with his own hand wrote the account, in which there were numberless small and great sums, both in gold and silver, together with the payment of the stipends of those already mentioned, pensions, and salaries, many of which would not have been incurred save for the legal suit. Additionally, one John Mankel D.Th. had died at the Curia, thus causing heavy loss and expense to the abbey. Br. Richard de Canterbury the treasurer, aged sixty-three, agreed with Geoffrey's calculation, adding that with his own hands he had disbursed £750 and more. Br. Peter de Wrotenham (Wrotham), a thirty-five year old monk, also corroborated Geoffrey, adding that he had himself disbursed £100 with his own hands. Thomas Catour, aged forty and more, likewise agreed with Geoffrey and added that a large sum of money had passed through his hands and he had rendered an account. Many other persons attested this and Itherius allegedly ruled that £1,210 should be paid by the archbishop to the religious. This is widely at variance with the £700 recorded in the *Literae Cantuarienses*.[22] Among the undecided business relating to Canterbury archbishops recorded in the register of Andreas Sapiti, the Florentine proctor resident at the Curia, was Mepham's appeal against Concoreto's sentence.[23]

In the event, not only did the archbishop die in a state of excommunication but with—whatever the true sum was—a massive debt for his executors to discharge. Following his sentence he retired to his manor of Mayfield in Sussex where on Sunday 22 August 1333, less than two months before his death, the sympathetic Bishop Hethe paid him a visit from his manor of Trottiscliffe in Kent and advised him to try every means to secure absolution. Mepham, clearly depressed, replied that he cared but little for absolution.[24] The *Instrumentum de morte* was published on 12 October. In it Mepham was said to have died at Mayfield about the hour of Vespers[25] in the presence of Masters Robert de Weston and Hamo de Tunstall, the priests Robert de Leveye, William de Canynggs, and William de Fyndon, as well as Thomas de Estune and a notary, John de Aumberleye. On the 15th, from Mayfield, a letter was sent to the prior notifying him of the anticipated advent to M. Robert de Weston, one of Mepham's long-serving clerks, to make the funeral arrangements.[26] The *Instrumentum de sepultura* followed on the 26th, when another notary, William de Natyndon, testified to having seen and touched the corpse.[27] Two days later on behalf of M. Peter de Durant, clerk of the priory, the *sede vacante* procuratorial document was read out in Christ Church Cathedral and the way was open for the election of Mepham's successor.

The contumacious archbishop was absolved after his death, so Bishop Hethe, who had witnessed his enthronement, endured his critical visitation, and consoled him in adversity, was now in a position to bury him on 26 October in St. Peter's chapel in the south aisle of Canterbury Cathedral choir. His shrine-like tomb, a black marble slab, now lies within a double screen across the entrance to St. Anselm's chapel not far from that of his successor John Stratford.[28] One of his executors, M. Laurence Fastolf, released £50 to the cathedral priory to augment the annual rent of 40s. for the celebration of his anniversary.[29]

Endnotes

1. Elected 1310, died 1334. *Heads of Religious Houses*, p.
2. In 1320 the parishioners of Faversham and Preston refused to pay certain tithes to the abbey and appealed to the apostolic see. The case was delegated to the prior of St. Gregory. Wright, *Reynolds*, p. 327 no. 45.
3. There is a full list of the abbey's spiritualities and temporalities in *Thorne*, 2161-
4. This is printed in *Lit. Cant.*, i. pp. 512-15 no. 483,.
5. These documents and other papal privileges for S. Augustine's are in *Monasticon* i. p. 126 *et seq*. Boniface's bulls are ibid., pp. 129-31.
6. The citation was supposed in error to have been delegated to an Aymer, rector of St. Julian, London (*Sancti Juliani Londoniae*). There is no such church, but Aymer de Rogesio is later mentioned as rector of St. Julian within the diocese of Sarlat in the Dordogne. *Thorne*, col. 2044.
7. The text has *Schordwich*, but this should perhaps be Shoreditch or Shordich. Is he identifiable as the renowned lawyer John de Shordich? If so he was an advocate in the court of Arches in 1328-9. His biography is in Emden, *Biog. Oxon.*, s.v. Shordich.
8. The process is the same as that for the more embracing condemnation detailed below.
9. 'Pars vero archiepiscopi fictitie proposuit recusare, enervare et declinare qua via posset jurisdictionem dicti judicis, talem materiam praetendens suspectivam, videlicet quod idem Itherius esset annualis pensionarius, pro nostris negotiis et auxiliis inpendendis et consiliarius specialis nimisque propicius & favens'. *Thorne*, col. 2042.
10. Thorne is imprecise about dates. There were parliaments at Westminster in November 1330 and September 1331, at both of which Bishops Stratford and Orleton were present and to which, of course, the archbishop was also summoned. It would seem to have been the latter.
11. 'Haec omnia idem archiepiscopus sibi male conscius in contemptum sanctitatis vestrae committere non expavit in gravem injuriam & praejudiciam monasterii vestri, quae quidem sunt in partibus multum notoria.' *Thorne*, col. 2043.
12. See App. 5.

[13] 'Si ista causa in Anglia potuisset terminasse, de facili archiepiscopi numerum triplicassent'. *Thorne*, col. 2046.

[14] *Lit. Cant.*, i. p. 467 no. 443.

[15] Ibid., pp. 482-3 no. 457.

[16] His appointment was somewhat irregular and emerged following a dispute between rival candidates. He occurs as prior in 1330 and was prior of Tavistock 1334-49. *Heads of Religious Houses*, pp. 234-5.

[17] *Thorne*, col. 2048. 'Peciit eciam attemptata per ipsum archiepiscopum irritari seu irrita esse et fuisse pronunciari'.

[18] *Lit. Cant.*, i. pp. 511-17 no. 483.

[19] ibid. pp. 517-19 no.

[20] It is interesting to note that Prior John, who may be the man indicated here, was apparently suspended following Archbishop Reynolds's visitation. *Heads of Religious Houses*, p. 358.

[21] The Latin here is *Godfridus*, Godfrey, but in the other instances below it is *Galfridus*, Geoffrey. I have used the latter.

[22] *Lit. Cant.*, i. pp. 515-6. Compare *Thorne*, cols. 2050-1.

[23] TNA (PRO) 31/9/17A, fos. 100r-103v: A 'Memorandum de negociis domini Cantuar' in Romana Curia' (cases which remained undecided) was brought to Sapiti by M. Laurence Fastolf, who became one of Mepham's executors. Mepham's appeal for revocation is the second item. Andreas Sapiti acted as proctor for Edward II and for Edward III until 1334, but after a period in England remained active at Avignon until his death in 1338. Sapiti's register has been edited by B. Bombi: *Il Registro di Andrea procuratore alla curia avignonese*, Ricerche dell'Istituto Storico Germanico di Roma 1, Rome 2007. See also TNA C70/1-7 Roman Rolls and *inter alia* Bombi, 'Andrea Sapiti: his Origins, and His Register as a Curial Proctor, *EHR* CXXIII (2008), 132-48.

[24] HR, fo. 66^r. 'Dominica die pro*xime* post festum Assumpcionis Beate Marie apud Maghfeld. archiepiscopum Symonem in magna tristicia sedentem videre porrexit ad consolendum eum et consulendum quod per omnes vias satageret a sentencia qua ligatus erat absolvi. Qui quidem archiepiscopus se parum curare de absolucione.'

25. The time of day differs from HR, for which see n. 26 below.
26. *HMCR Var. Coll.* 1, Muniments of the Dean and Chapter of Canterbury, p. 215.
27. CCA DCc Reg. Q, fo. 187r-v al. 192. The opening rubric of this section reads: 'Processus postulacionis in ecclesia Christi Cant. facte de venerabili patre Johanne [Stratford] ... '
28. HR, fo. 66v. 'Die Martis in aurora Simon archiepiscopus Cant. apud Maghfeld obiit, quem episcopus Roffensis die Martis post xiiii dies obitus sui in ecclesia Cant. sepelivit'.
29. *Anglia Sacra*, i. p. 59.

Chapter Seven

FINAL ASSESSMENT

Simon Mepham occupied the metropolitan see for five years, four months and seventeen days.[1] No Canterbury archbishop had spent so short a period in office since Robert Kilwardby (1273-8), nor until the Black Death carried off John Offord and Thomas Bradwardine in 1348-9 would another do so.

CONCERN FOR POLITICAL AND SOCIAL REFORM

Undoubtedly what Mepham lacked was caution, vital at the time of political upheaval. To this was added a determination to ride roughshod over privileges which impeded the exercise of his metropolitan jurisdiction. His action in 1328 when he thrust himself into the political maelstrom was ill-considered, and the Christmas season inappropriate, as the usually reticent Hamo de Hethe was anxious to make clear to his superior. What is more it was all too early in the new regime. Mepham had neither the political awareness nor the legal acumen of an Orleton or a Stratford who were conscious of their limitations. The latter was certainly a strong proponent of Earl Henry of Lancaster, but wise enough to withdraw when things became too hot. So far as is known, Stratford as his itinerary demonstrates, unlike Hethe, did respond initially to Mepham's call late in 1328 for help from the episcopate for his programme of constitutional reform but did not then proceed northwards towards Bedford. As has been shown, on 16 December at Otford Mepham launched his exhortatory mandate *Iustus et misericors Dominus visitans in verberibus* calling for prayers and processions on behalf of the peace of church and realm and settlement of dissensions in return for a 40 days' indulgence. Here indeed was a political as well as a pastoral move.[2]

Mepham's heart was in the right place, as his political manifesto at the time demonstrates, but he was up against powerful forces: an insurgent queen who had exhibited iron determination, and Mortimer who was in process of establishing his dominant position in the government. Mepham's reported pusillanimity at Bedford brought a degree of ignominy and was an object lesson in politics that he did not forget. To a degree, of course, he was unlucky in the time of his promotion. The king was a minor and the Mortimer-Isabella regime was attempting to consolidate itself after a period of civil war and political infighting. There were those who could not adjust themselves to the radically new situation, recalled their oaths of fidelity with varying degrees of shame, and hankered after the old king, despite his ineffectiveness. What might be considered regularity was not re-established until after the *coup d'état* of October 1330 which dislodged Mortimer, removed the queen from political influence, and left the king untrammelled.

EDWARD II's ALLEGED SURVIVAL

It is noteworthy that Mepham's name, unlike that of William Melton, the contemporary archbishop of York (1317-40) does not come to the surface when rumours of the king's continued existence were rife during 1329 and the early part of 1330. Doubtless this was in part because he had not experienced the same relationship with the former king as some others such as his northern counterpart had done. Also, perhaps, he had no wish for further embroilment with factions and the certainty of government reprisals. Melton, the evidence argues, allowed himself to be convinced, not only that Edward of Caernarfon was alive and still in England,[3] but also that he could receive external help towards gaining his freedom. Indicative of this belief is the fortuitous survival of a letter sent by Melton to his 'cher vallet' and 'cher ami' Simon de Swaneslond or Swanlond, citizen of London, who was in fact the mayor at the time, asking him to arrange delivery to the captive of a chest of expensive clothes. The letter, which survived initially in the Swanlond archives, became incorporated into those of the Newdegate (Newdigate) family at Arbury Hall near Nuneaton following a marriage with the heiress of the Swanlands, and is now deposited in the Warwickshire Record Office. It is dated from the archiepiscopal manor of Cawood in Yorkshire on the morrow of St. Hilary, that is 14 January, presumably 1330.[4]

Widespread rumours of Edward's survival flourished elsewhere, particularly in Kent, and the anxiety of Edmund of Woodstock, the earl of Kent, to release or even to reinstate his half-brother led to his death on 19 March 1330. It has to be remembered, though, that while Archbishop Melton and Bishops Gravesend and Hethe had been reluctant to accept the change of king, it was only the sceptical Hethe who did not allow himself to be taken in by the widespread rumour that he remained alive. This, the local Rochester chronicler thought, was merely a scheme fostered by agents of the queen and of Roger Mortimer to deceive the credulous into believing that the king's father had not died after all, in order to extort money from Edward of Caernarfon's well-wishers: Bishop Gravesend, Archbishop Melton, and William (Digepet?) abbot of Langdon, among many others.[5] Under this pretext much money was in fact raised and dissidents kept under restraint.

PARTICIPATION IN NATIONAL AFFAIRS

The witness lists for royal charters between January 1330 and January 1332 show that Mepham witnessed only rarely, thirteen times in all. Furthermore, unlike Bishop John Stratford, whose attendances shot up following Mortimer's fall, his remained at only four between 19th October 1330 and the January 24th 1332. But, of course, Stratford had become chancellor at the end of November 1330.[6]

A notable state function took place on 18 February 1330 when Mepham crowned the already pregnant Queen Philippa in Westminster Abbey and afterwards dined at the nearby royal palace.[7] In the following April, some two years after the Bedford fiasco, Mepham himself entertained the king. The circumstances could not have been more different. Edward III was abroad In 1331 between the 4th and the 20th of April for the performance of homage to King Philip VI. On his return Mepham received him at his manor of Wingham in Kent.[8]

Another aspect of the archbishop's interests, which arose naturally from his theological training and pastoral concern, as well as from his local origins, was the grant of an indulgence for all who should pray for the soul of the contemporary Kentish poet William de Shoreham, the vicar of Chart near Leeds. Shoreham's work is contained in BL Add. MS 17376 and was published by the Early English Text Society in 1902. It concerns itself with doctrinal matters and with praise of the Virgin.[9]

JURISDICTIONAL DISPUTES

Mepham kept clear of further contentious political involvement but, as has been demonstrated, he was soon to fall into an abyss of an even more damaging kind. Throughout the Canterbury province, as elsewhere, there were intermittent jurisdictional disputes. Even in the fourteenth century demarcation could still be a source of friction. One such instance was the exercise by the metropolitan of *sede vacante* jurisdiction in suffragan sees. On this occasion at Norwich, as we have seen, there was an amicable settlement without resort to a legal contest, as Prior Eastry had advised.

Bishop Grandisson did not forget the way in which he and his diocese had been treated both by Mepham and the Court of Canterbury and bemoaned the fact that this continued under his successor, Stratford.[10] This doubtless helps to explain the acephalous irascible entry occurring earlier in the Exeter bishop's register.[11]

Throughout Mepham's tenure of the primacy there was acrimonious conflict with the northern primate about the latter's raising of his metropolitical cross within the southern province. This proved particularly awkward when the two prelates were summoned to parliament. While Mepham cannot be blamed for the initiation of this unsalutary and often unseemly dispute, he is not known to have made any move to resolve the matter. When he unsuccessfully attempted to secure the support of his suffragans for a mass withdrawal from parliament, it was argued that such refusal to attend might entail confiscation of his temporalities. Nothing daunted, he foolishly sought to pose as a willing martyr and to ape St. Thomas.[12]

THE DOWNWARD SLIDE TO EXCOMMUNICATION

Quite why Mepham allowed himself to be swallowed up in the legal morass which ended in his excommunication is now almost incomprehensible. A hint may be provided by the addition he made to his title. In October 1328 he used the usual 'Simon permissione divina Cantuariensis archiepiscopus, tocius Anglie primas', and regularly did so. But much later, in 1332 and 1333, he added '*apostolice sedis legatus*'. It could be that he considered this addition to be an indication that he was not subject to the interference of other papal legates, in line with his successful petition while at Avignon, the more particularly as he had lodged an appeal. The bull of July 1328 conceded that, in order to prevent any derogation from the archbishop's status, while in places and manors in which he happened to be staying, he should not be compelled to respond to mandates from the apostolic see or its officials which, under penalty of excommunication, suspension or interdict, demanded his response in distant places.[13] One can only assume that this stubborn character was not well advised by his legal clerks, and so blundered from one impasse to another. The violence at Slindon was the last straw. An objective assessment of the evidence, as presented on both sides, can hardly fail to conclude that the archbishop's claim to have known nothing of what was going on does not ring true. Of course, he may not have initiated the violence, he swore he did not, but his *familia* must have felt in the heat of the moment that they knew the archbishop's mind in the rejection of the citation. The matter then got out of hand as might have been expected in the circumstances. This led Mepham on a downward course as he struggled to avoid recognition of the actions of the papal legate Itherius de Concoreto. This final débâcle can be added to the earlier ones of the Maidstone provision and the siege of Exeter. The consequence was that a disillusioned Mepham closed his rule in a state of excommunication. His attempts to exercise political influence and his reckless determination to uphold what he considered to be the inalienable rights of his metropolitan see had ended in disaster and personal obloquy.

The last office that, as executor, Fastolf could perform for his master's spiritual benefit was to assign fifty pounds to the Cathedral priory for the purchase of annual rents to provide forty shillings for the support of his anniversary.

Endnotes

[1] BL Add. MS. 6159, fo. 2v.

[2] CCA DCc Reg. I, fos. 428v-9r.

[3] The story that Edward escaped from Corfe by way of Ireland to the continent, visited the pope and ended up in the guise of a penitential hermit stems from a copy of a letter under the name of Manuel de Flisco (Fieschi) incorporated in a manuscript volume now at Montpellier in the *Archives d'Herault*. It has been much discussed, among others by Cuttino and Lyman, 'Where is Edward II' and Haines, '*Edwardus Redivivus*'. The letter is illustrated in Mortimer, 'The Greatest Traitor', opp. p. 205. The original is marked 'vacat' in the margin. This does not appear in the illustration nor has it been mentioned other than by the present writer. The internet essay by Ian Mortimer 'A Note on the Deaths of Edward' (www.ianmortimer.com/Edward II/ death), details the literature on the topic up to 2006 and from his *parti pris* position is dismissive of any historian who considers that the king died at Berkeley in 1327.

[4] Warwickshire Record Office CR 136/C2027. Cited by permission of the Record Office and the owners of the MS. Transcription in Haines, 'Sumptuous Apparel for a Royal Prisoner'.

[5] HR, fo. 55v. '…quod rex pater viveret, ad cuius vite assercionem per reginam et Rogerum de Mortuo Mari ut dicebatur quidam procurati [missi?] fuerunt ad denunciandum Edmundo comiti Kancie quod frater eius viveret, similiter archiepiscopo Eboracensi, Londoniensi episcopo, et aliis benevolis regis patris datum fuit intelligi in dolo quod rex esset vivus et totum hoc ad sciendum et extorquendum quis vel qui benevol[i] fuerint regis patris et propter hoc columpniarentur et punirentur pecuniam dando.' Compare TCC R 5 41, fo. 128r (al. 129). His supposed incarceration at Corfe at this time is described in Baker, *Chronicon*, pp. 43-4, who considered the 'Kent affair' to be wholly 'falsum et fantasium'. *Ibid*. Notes, pp. 220-5, containing an even longer account from the English *Brut* chronicle.

6   TNA (PRO) C53 Charter Rolls. The calendar does not include witnesses and originally I consulted the PRO typescript no/25/50. Mortimer, *Edward III*, Appendix 4, has now printed the relevant details.

7   HR, fo. 56r; *Annales Paulini*, p. 349.

8   Parkin, 'Wingham a Medieval Town', p. 65, citing A Hussey, *Some Account of the Parish Church of Wingham*, 1891.

9   Konrath, *The Poems of William of Shoreham*.

10   *Exeter Reg. Grandisson*, p. 278: 'licet odium illud predecessoris vestri ac Curie Cantuariensis, quod cum persona extinctum fuisse credebamus, contra nos, ut Dominacionem vestram penitus non latet, minus juste conceptum, et hucusque—quod dolenter referimus—per Ministros ejusdem inhumaniter continuatum . . .'

11   Ibid. pp. 195-6. The addressee is not recorded but it begins 'Licet calliditate vulpina, cum serpentini anfractibus, maliciosam et Deo odibilem contra nos et statum nostrum, ac ecclesie nostre et dignitatis episcopalis debitam obedienciam in anime tue dampnacionem et fidelitatis tue lesionem' and much more in the same unbridled vein. It has been suggested that it was written to Archbishop Mepham. It is in any case clear that Grandisson was outraged against both the archbishop and the Canterbury court.

12   See *EA*, pp. 99-102.

13   Reg. Aven. 31, fo. 122v, 14 July 1328. This privilege is copied on p. 4 of CCA ChAnt/A/36/ii, somewhat incongruously among miscellaneous cases in the archiepiscopal court.

Appendix 1

ACTA OF ARCHBISHOP MEPHAM 1328-1333

▶ [11 Dec. 1327. Election by 'way of compromise' to Canterbury; 27 May 1328. Election presented to Mepham at Chichester, where he was a resident canon. Papal confirmation; 5 June consecration at Avignon and delivery of the 'pallium' four days later. CCA DCc Reg. Q, fo. 127^v; *EA*, pp. 30-31].

¶ 19 June 1328 Avignon. Commission for Edmund de Mepham to act as Official or vicar-general. CCA Dcc Reg. Q, fo. 129^r. This commission is not mentioned in Churchill, *Canterbury Administration*, but see 'Ornaments' (App. 4).

▶ [7-8 July. Above commission and papal bulls read out in Canterbury chapter. CCA Dcc Reg. Q, fo. 127^v, 'Ornaments' (App. 4).]

▶ [17 July [1328]. Bishop Stratford responds to abp.'s claim [no date] to appoint a nun to Romsey abbey. Winchester Reg. Stratford, fo. 37^v, edn. no. 367.

▶ [5 Sept. 1328. Mepham takes ship at Antwerp in Brabant and disembarks at Dover, proceeding by way of Chatham, Rochester and Gravesend, where he crossed the River Thames. CCA DCc Reg. Q, fo.129^v, HR, fo. 51^v. See App. 4].

▶ [25 Sept. 1328. Visits St. Paul's and makes a 'parva collacio', *Ann. Paulini*, p. 342.]

⁋ 29 Sept. 1328 Mortlake. Mandate to Prior Eastry to hold an enquiry as to the health of the provost of Wingham and if necessary to provide a coadjutor. *Lit. Cant.* 1, p. 269.

⁋ —[1328]. Letter to Henry, rector of Patching, deanery of Tarring in abp.'s immediate jurisdiction, giving his decision in a suit between the rector and a parishioner concerning the taking of coppice wood, brushwood and ash (*silva cedua, subsoscus, fraxinus*) within the parish. ChAnt/A/36ii, pp. 1-2.

⁋ 28 Oct. 1328 Darnford, Suffolk. Commission for exchange of Teynham vicarage, Canterbury diocese, and St. Andrew, Hertford. *Reg. Burghersh* ii, no. 2529.

⁋ 29 Nov. 1328 Mayfield. Summons to provincial council at St. Paul's. Winchester Reg. Stratford 43^r, edn. no. 441; *Records of Convocation III*, pp. 101-3.

⁋ 30 Nov. 1328 Mayfield. Appointment of Br. Peter, bishop of Corbavia, to ordain in Canterbury Cathedral on Saturday in Embertide (17 December), both those monks presented by the precentor and beneficed clerks of the city, diocese, and immediate jurisdictions presented by the commissary-general with the assistance of the official of the archdeacon of Canterbury. Printed 'Ornaments', p. 371, from CCA DCc Reg. Q, fo. 130^r.

⁋ 16 Dec. 1328 Otford. *Iustus et misericors Dominus visitans in verberibus.* Mandate for prayers and processions on behalf of the peace of church and realm and settlement of dissensions. 40 days' indulgence. CCA DCc Reg. I, fos. 428^v-9^r. Compare *Iustus et misericors Dominus in omnibus viis suis* at 23 April

▶ [21 Dec. 1328. *Supplicacio prelatorum comitum et baronum et tocius communitatis London' facta domino regi in festo Sancti Thome apostoli anno domin MoCCCmoxxviii*]. CCA DCc Reg. I, fos. 427^{r-v}; *Lit. Cant.* 3, pp. 414-6.

⁋ 23 Dec. 1329 Letter [summarised] to the king reminding him of engagements at the Salisbury parliament and of his coronation oath to maintain the laws and customs of England. *P. & M.R. Rolls*, p. 84.

▶ [22 Jan. 1329. Enthronement at Canterbury following Bedford débâcle.]

Archbishop Simon Mepham 1328-1333: A Boy Amongst Men

¶ 9 or 10 March 1329 Wingham. Mandate for enquiry as to the status of St. Giles chapel with respect to the vicarage of St. Leonard's Bristol, on which matters Abp. Winchelsey had given a ruling. *Worcester Reg. Orleton*, no. 574.

¶ 10 March 1329 Wingham. Proxy for recovery of fruits of canonry of Lyon (*manerium de Quinciaco*) assigned to the abp. Ducarel, fo. 53ʳ (from autograph of Matthew Parker). Printed Wilkins, *Concilia* 2, p. 554.

¶ 16 April 1329 Charing. Certificate of the exchange carried out between John de Woodhouse, rector of Wittersham, Canterbury diocese, and Richard de Brampton, rector of Earl's Barton. By commission of the bishop of Lincoln, Henry Burghersh, he has instituted Woodhouse to the latter benefice. *Reg. Burghersh* ii, no. 1366.

¶ 20 May 1329 Charing. Commission for exchange of benefices of East Lavant (exempt deanery, Chichester diocese) and Chesterford (London diocese). *London Reg. Stephen Gravesend*, p. 289 n.

¶ 13 June 1329 Otford. Mandate against countenancing the bearing of the metropolitan cross by William Melton, abp. of York, expected shortly to pass through the province of Canterbury. *Worcester Reg. Orleton*, no. 738.

¶ 2 July 1329 Otford. Mandate against the bearing of the cross by Abp. Melton, said to be in the neighbourhood of Windsor. Lincoln Reg. Burghersh V, fo. 419ʳ⁻ᵛ.

¶ [21 July 1329—. Confirmation of Ralph of Shrewsbury's election. *Bath & Wells Reg. Salopia*, pp. 11-12, nos. 39-40.]

¶ 23 July 1329 Mortlake. Grant of 40 days' indulgence for those praying for the souls of Mepham's parents and the benefactors of Meopham church. *Registrum Roffense* 2, p. 777.

¶ 25 July 1329 Horton-by-Windsor. Further mandate [see under 2 July] against countenancing the bearing of his cross in Canterbury province by Abp. Melton. *Worcester Reg. Orleton*, no. 742.

¶ 7 Aug. 1329 Mortlake. Mandate for the consecration at Canterbury on 3 September of the bp. of Bath & Wells, Ralph of Shrewsbury, received 10 Aug. by Burghersh. Lincoln Reg. Burghersh V, fo. 420ᵛ and see below.

¶ 7 August 1329 Mortlake. Letter complaining that Edmund de Neville has intruded into the church of Great Horkesley (Essex) by lay force and in defiance of the sentences of the Court of Canterbury, preventing the rector, John de Coule, from gaining access to his church or the fruits. Request for action by the sheriff of Essex.

¶ 12 Aug. 1329 Croydon. Mandate for implementation of the mandates against the anti-pope, Br. Peter of Corbaria (Nicholas V, 1328-30), and his supporter, Lewis of Bavaria. *Bath & Wells Reg. Salopia*, p. 13 no. 48; Lincoln Reg. Burghersh V, fo. 421^v. For Corbaria see *Murimuth*, pp. 59 n. 7, 61 n. 4.

¶ 3 Sept. 1329 Canterbury. Consecration of Ralph of Shrewsbury as bp. of Bath & Wells. HR, fo. 53^r; *Ann. Paulini*, p. 347.

¶ 9 Sept. 1329 Mayfield. Recitation of custom whereby newly appointed abp. can nominate to a canonry or prebend. Proposes his clerk Master Laurence Fastolf. *Bath & Wells Reg. Salopia*, pp. 2-3; Ducarel, fo. 18^{r-v} (Lambeth Reg. Album).

¶ 14 Sept. 1329 Mayfield. Further mandate urging Bp. Orleton to respond to that of March concerning the chapel of St. Giles. *Worcester Reg. Orleton*, no. 575.

▶ [2 Oct. 1329 Rochester. Visitation of the Benedictine chapter. HR, fo.53^{r-v}; *Rochester Reg. Hethe* 1, p. 389.]

¶ 6 Oct. 1329 Cliffe-by-Higham (Kent). Mandate to Bp. Ralph of Shrewsbury for copying the process against Peter de Corbaria and Lewis of Bavaria. *Bath & Wells Reg. Salopia*, p. 13, no. 48.

¶ 1 Nov. 1329 Mortlake. Mandate reciting bull of John XXII concerning the first fruits of churches and monasteries, Avignon. Ducarel, fo. 22^r; *Bath & Wells Reg. Salopia*, p.16 no. 60; Wilkins, *Concilia* 2, p. 557.

¶ 5 Nov. 1329 Mortlake. Mandate to the officers responsible for the temporalities of the archbishopric to observe the composition between Abp. Boniface and the prior and chapter. *Lit. Cant.* 1, p. 300 and cf. 304-5.

¶ 5 Nov. 1329 Mayfield. Commission to Br. Peter de Corbavia (Corbaviensis) to celebrate oders at Canterbury. CCA DCc Reg.Q, fo. 130^v.

Archbishop Simon Mepham 1328-1333: A Boy Amongst Men

⁋ 8 Dec. 1329 Mortlake. The abp. certifies that he has executed the commission of the bishop of Winchester (John Stratford) for the exchange of the benefices of Hayes, in his immediate jurisdiction, and of Amport, Winchester diocese. Winchester Reg. Stratford, fo. 117^r, edn. no. 1229.

⁋ 15 Jan. 1330 Otford. Lincoln Reg. Burghersh V, fo. 400^v. Mandate against Abp. of York's elevation of his primatial cross in Canterbury province, received 19 Jan. at Old Temple, London, by Bp. Burghersh

⁋ 3 Feb. 1330 Mortlake. In response to a royal writ of 26 Jan. 1330 from Eltham, requiring the meeting of parliament at Winchester on 11 Mar., which he received on 2 Feb., the abp. summoned the clergy before him in Winchester Cathedral on 13 Mar. 1330. *Records of Convocation III*, pp. 115-16, where the reference is given as Reg. Burghersh II [=LAO V, VB], fo. 129^r, but I have not found that entry in either register. In Reg. V, fo. 403^{r-v}, the royal writ is dated 26 Feb. 1330 likewise from Eltham. See 11 Feb. below.

⁋ 10 Feb. 1330 Mortlake. Mandate against the Abp. of York's bearing of his cross within Canterbury province. Winchester Reg. Stratford, fo. 54^v (received 24 Feb. 1330 at Esher), edn. no. 551. See also 20 February and 10 December 1330.

⁋ 10 Feb. 1330 Mortlake. Dimission of Bishop Hethe from the charges brought against him at visitation. *Rochester Reg. Hethe* 1, pp. 424-8.

⁋ 11 Feb. 1330 Mortlake. Mandate for convocation at Winchester 11 March in response to a royal writ. Lincoln Reg. Burghersh V, fo. 403^{r-v}. The archbishop's mandate sent through that of the dean of the province, Bishop Gravesend of London, dated 14 February, was received by Burghersh at the Old Temple, London, on the 17th. The royal mandate is recorded to have been dated from Eltham 26 Feb. (*recte* Jan.). See 3 Feb. above.

▶ [18 Feb. 1330 Westminster. Mepham crowns Queen Philippa in the abbey and afterwards dines at the royal palace. HR, fo. 56^r; *Annales Paulini*, p. 349].

⁋ 20 Feb. 1330 Mortlake. Mandate against the Abp. of York's bearing of his cross within Canterbury province. Coventry and Lichfield Reg. Northburgh, fo. 107^r

⁋ 22 Mar. 1330 Mortlake. Commission for M. Robert de Worth, canon of Salisbury, to act as *custos* and Official of Salisbury diocese *sede vacante*. Salisbury Reg. Wyville 2, fo. ii^r

⁋ 22 Mar. 1330 Mortlake. Mandate to the dean and chapter of Salisbury to render obedience to the *custos*. Ibid.

⁋ 24 Mar. 1330 Mortlake. Summons to convocation at Lambeth 16 April in response to a royal writ reeived 21 March. Canterbury Reg. I, fo. 432^v; Lincoln Reg. Burghersh V, fo. 429^{r-v}; *Records of Convocation III*, pp. 117-19.

⁋ 12 April 1330 Mortlake. Mandate against the abp. of York's carrying of his cross in the province. He is believed to be intending travelling across Lincoln diocese. Lincoln Reg. Burghersh V, fo. 430^{r-v}.

⁋ 30 May 1330. Letter to Edward III declaring that Hugh de Burghton, priest, indicted for stealing horses, has proceeded to purgation. Request for the return to him of his goods. TNA (PRO) SC8 /197/

⁋ 19 June 1330 Mortlake. Letter concerning the appointment to Charlton Mackrell (Som). Thomas de Essche has been presented by the true patrons, although Richard de Middleton claims collation and induction on the abp.'s authority during vacancy (Bp. Ralph of Shrewsbury was consecrated 3 Sept. 1329). *Bath & Wells. Reg. Salopia*, pp. 50-1 nos. 199-201.

⁋ 27 June [1330] Harrow manor. Mepham presides over the audience court. The parties in dispute, William de Pynnore and John de Barnevyle, agree to abide by the award of six persons, three to be nominated by each, and swore on the archiepiscopal cross, under a monetary penalty to be disbursed in alms, to abide by their ruling. Cant. ChAnt/A/36ii, p. 42.

⁋ 20 July 1330 Mortlake. Mandate for inspection of papal letters with respect to quadrennial tenth. *Bath & Wells Reg. Salopia*, p.55 no. 216.

⁋ 23 July 1330 Mortlake. Mandate as collector of the quadrennial tenth to the abbot of Faversham, appointed as his sub-collector, reciting a papal bull for its collection. *Lit. Cant.* 1, pp. 322-33.

¶ 14 Aug. 1330 Saltwood. Norwich *sede vacante* composition temp. Prior William de Claxton (1326-44). Ducarel, fos. 33^r-51^v (from Reg. Album and Canterbury Reg. Islep, fos. 327^r-328^v, 338^{r-v}), NRO box 'Confirmation and settlements of peculiar jurisdiction', nos. 2757, 3854-5. The letters patent of Bishop Ayrminne are printed in *Canterbury Admin.* 2, pp. 64-9 from Reg. Islep fo. 338. Prior William Claxton and the Norwich chapter confirmed the composition 4 August 1330, the bishop's approval following on the 26th at Canterbury (NRO. loc. cit. no. 3853, and entry below). The Canterbury chapter added its confirmation on 29 Aug. This composition is cited in BRECP, p. 495, as DCN 42/2/4. In *Lit. Cant.* 1, pp. 316-7, the prior of Canterbury's preliminary approval of Mepham's composition is dated the feast of Saints Peter and Paul (29 June 1330).

¶ [26 Aug. 1330 Canterbury, date of Bishop Ayrminne's sealing]. Confirmation of the Norwich *sede vacante* composition. Printed *Canterbury Administration*, ii. pp. 64-9 from Cant. Reg. Islep, fo. 338^r.

¶ 12 Oct. 1330 Mortlake. Commission to the bishop of Lincoln for exchange of the churches of Little Staughton and Deal, Canterbury diocese. *Reg. Burghersh* ii, no. 2051.

¶ 10 Sept. Wingham The archbishop relays Itherius de Concoreto's mandate for the collection of the tenth.

¶ 3 Nov. 1330 Slindon. Mandate to the bishop of Lincoln against the carrying by the abp. of York of his primatial cross within his diocese. Lincoln Reg. Burghersh V, fo. 439^v-440^r.

¶ 24 Nov. 1330 Shalford (*Schaldeford*) (Surr.), Winchester diocese. Mandate for the execution of the letters of the papal nuncio, Itherius de Concoreto requiring citation of collectors of quadrennial tenth. *Bath & Wells Reg. Salopia*, p. 60, no.

¶ 8 Dec. 1330 Lambeth. Mandate directed against the abp. of York who has had his cross carried before him in Canterbury province. *Worcester Reg. Orleton*, no. 793.

¶ 10 Dec. 1330 Lambeth. Further mandate against the abp. of York against his carrying the cross. Winchester Reg. Stratford, fo. 54^v, edn. no. 552; Lincoln Reg. Burghersh V, fo. 442^{r-v}, 443^v. Apparently it was to this mandate and others (*proximis precedentibus*) that Bp. Burghersh responded on 30 Jan. 1331 from London, although the marginal rubric reads: *litterarum . . . certificatarum ad festum Purificacionis Beate Marie.*

¶ 15 Dec. 1330 Lambeth. Dispensation for the bishop of Bath & Wells (Ralph of Shrewsbury) to go on pilgrimage (*sanctorum limina*). *Bath & Wells Reg. Salopia*, p. 65, no. 258.

¶ *post* 21 Mar. 1331 Mepham's oath excusing himself from responsibility for the fracas at Slindon on that day *Thorne*, col. 2045.

¶ 13 Apr. 1331 Mortlake Letter to the subprior of Canterbury to the effect that he will be in the chapter house for the election of the prior [allegedly on the following Tuesday, but see below]. *Lit, Cant.* 1, pp. 360-1.

▶ [20 Apr. 1331 Wingham. Entertains Edward III. E. W. Parkin, 'Wingham, A Medieval Town', p. 6; *Foedera* (Hague edn.) 2, iii. p. 65.]

¶ 25-26 Apr. 1331 Canterbury. Process at the time of Richard de Oxenden's election. His appointment announced by the archbishop to the chapter (26th). CCA Dcc Reg. G., fo. 22^v; Ducarel, fos.15^v-17^r (Reg. Album).

¶ 26 June 1331 Edington (Wilts.), Salisbury diocese. Confirmation of the election of Br. Richard Marny (*recte* Maury) as abbot of Milton (1331-52). Ducarel fo. 32^{r-v} (from Reg. Album); *Heads of Religious Houses*, p.

¶ 29 June 1331 Longbridge Deverill, Wilts., mandate for implementation of Itherius de Concoreto's mandate for the rendering by subcollectors of accounts for the papal quadrennial. Lincoln Reg. Burghersh V, fos. 448^v-9^r

¶ 24 July 1331 Frampton (Dors.), Salisbury diocese. Mandate warning of his intended visitation of Wells cathedral on 16 Sept. 1331. *Bath & Wells Reg. Salopia*, p. 68, no. 274.

¶ 7 Aug. 1331 Chardstock (Dev.), Salisbury diocese, Cornwall Record Office, AR/1/1029

Archbishop Simon Mepham 1328-1333: A Boy Amongst Men

⁋ 8 Aug. 1331 Chardstock (Dev.), Letter informing Ralph of Shrewsbury of his intended visitation of his diocese on Monday after the Nativity of the BVM (9 Sept.). *Bath & Wells Reg. Salopia*, p. 70, no. 280.

⁋ 17 Aug. 1331 Chardstock. The abp. has heard that at Westminster parliament on 30 Sept. the abp. of York intends to arrive with cross raised. [Bp. Stratford replies that York has not come and that he was not tepid in his execution of the abp.'s mandate.], Winchester Reg. Stratford, fo. 64^v, edn. no. 638; Lincoln Reg. Burghersh V, fo. 451^{r-v}. Also *London Reg. Stephen Gravesend*, pp. 250-1 inchoate and undated.

⁋ 1 Sept. 1331 Chardstock (Dev.). *Exeter Reg. Grandisson*, pp. 259-60, nos 206-7. Letter to Bp. Ralph of Shrewsbury about John de Dyneham's wish for reconciliation. He has sent William de Crowthorne LL.D. to the bishop.

⁋ 7 Sept. 1331 Long Sutton (Som.). Reply about the above John de Dyneham, now likened to a prodigal. *Exeter Reg. Grandisson*, p. 260, no. 208.

▶ [16 Sept. 1331. Visitation of Wells Cathedral, Bath & Wells diocese. Bp. Ralph of Shrewsbury subsequently (3 Aug. 1332) required the provost to remedy defects in accordance with Mepham's statute of 1329.]

⁋ 23 Oct. 1331 Mortlake. As sole executor of a papal bull permitting him to grant dispensation for a marriage within the fourth degree of affinity, he commits his powers to Bp. Hethe. *Rochester Reg. Hethe* 1, pp. 469-

⁋ 25 Oct. 1331 Waverley (Surr.), Winchester diocese. Mandate to compel rendering of accounts of papal tenths. Lincoln Reg. Burghersh V, fo. 452^v.

⁋ 3 Nov. 1331 Beaumes [Bp. Orleton's Berkshire manor], Salisbury diocese. Letter informing Orleton of a judgement in the Canterbury Audience Court with respect to Beaconsfield church, Lincoln diocese. [Orleton had received a commission to institute from Bishop Burghersh.] *Worcester Reg. Orleton*, nos. 860-1.

⁋ 20 Nov.[1331] West Monkton (Som.), Bath & Wells diocese. Mandate to enquire concerning those who inflicted damage on the archbishop's ministers and servants during visitation at Glastonbury Abbey. *Bath & Wells Reg. Salopia*, pp. 77-8, no. 234.

▶ [*Mepham kept Christmas 1331 at Wiveliscombe, Som.*, Baker, *Chronicon*, p. 50; *Murimuth*, p. 65.]

⁋ [Apr.] 1332—Commission to Bp. Hethe for exchange between the rectors of Beddington [John de Wyndesore], Surr., and Wickhambreux [Richard de Castro], Kent, Canterbury diocese. Winchester Reg. Stratford fo. 132^v, edn. no. 1401; *Rochester Reg. Hethe* 1, pp. 514-15.

⁋ 11 Jan. 1332 Wiveliscombe (Som.), Bath & Wells diocese. Mandate against the abp. of York's carrying of his cross in the province. Lincoln Reg. Burghersh V, fo. 458r-v; cf. *Bath & Wells Reg. Salopia*, pp. 88-9 no. 366.

⁋ 11 Jan. 1332 Wiveliscombe. Mandate to Bp. Ralph of Shrewsbury under threat of suspension to apprehend Ela wife of Sir Robert FitzPain. *Bath & Wells Reg. Salopia*, pp. 87-8, no. 362.

⁋ 29 January 1332 Wiveliscombe (Som.). Penance imposed on Ela la Payne for adultery with knights and even with clerks in holy orders. Winchester Reg. Stratford, fos. 70^{r-v}, edn. no. 682.

⁋ 10 Feb. 1332 Wiveliscombe (Som.). Mandate reciting that of the king for a parliament at Westminster. Lincoln Reg. Burghersh V, fo. 457^r; *Bath & Wells Reg. Salopia*, pp. 88-9, no. 366; *Lit. Cant.* 1, pp. 438-40. [Mepham, according to Prior Eastry, was not going to be there on the first day on account of the abp. of York's arrival. *Lit. Cant.* 1, p. 440.]

⁋ —Feb. 1332 Chardstock (Dev.), Exeter diocese. The abp. reaffirms against the prior his version of the summons (above). *Lit. Cant.* 1, pp. 441-2.

⁋ 22 Feb. 1332 Croscombe (Dev.), Mandate to Bp. Ralph of Shrewsbury directing him to inhibit on pain of excommunication those obstructing his visitation. *Bath & Wells Reg. Salopia*, pp. 90-1 no. 373 and see also p. 83, no. 332.

⁋ 28 Feb. 1332 Tarrant Monkton (Dors.), Salisbury diocese. Response to the prior and convent of Canterbury affirming the correctness of his summons to parliament. *Lit.Cant.* 1, pp. 442-3.

¶ 6 April 1332 Newark Priory (Surr.), Winchester diocese. Mepham authorises the prior of Canterbury to hear the confessions of his monks and to absolve them with certain cases excepted. [The prior was to declare that the powers conceded were too limited.] *Lit. Cant.* 1, pp. 450-1.

¶ 12 April 1332 Mayfield (Kent). Mepham authorises Bp. Stratford to carry out an exchange of the benefices of Milsted (Kent) and Dogmersfield (Hants.), Winchester Reg. Stratford fo. 133^v, edn. no. 1417.

¶ 14 April 1332 Hinton (Dors.), Salisbury diocese. Excommunication of Ela la Payne who had not performed the penance imposed upon her [see 29 January 1332] with a warning to the faithful not to communicate with her. Winchester Reg. Stratford, fos. 70^v-71^r, edn. no. 683.

¶ 17 April 1332 Kingston (Dors.). Mepham explains the scope of the above commission of 6 April. *Lit. Cant.* 1, pp. 451-3.

¶ 19 May 1332 Wiveliscombe (Som.). Letter to Bp. Hethe regarding his exercise of episcopal functions on his behalf and request that he try to appease the disaffection of the monks of Christ Church towards their new prior (Richard de Oxenden, elected 25 April 1331, see above). This problem not noted in *BRECP*. Rochester Reg. Hethe 1, pp. 516-17.

¶ 22 May 1332 Wiveliscombe. Commission to Bp. Hethe to celebrate orders and to carry out other episcopal functions on behalf of the archbishop. *Rochester Reg. Hethe* 1, pp. 516-

¶ 22 May 1332 Wiveliscombe. Appointment of six persons, including William de Mundham D.Th., Thomas [de Canterbury] the abp.'s commissary-general, and Thomas de Wouhope his treasurer, as examiners of those presented to Bp. Hethe, the Rochester diocesan, deputed to hold an ordination on the abp.'s behalf. [The ordination took place in the monastic infirmary at Canterbury on Saturday the vigil of Trinity, 13 June.]. *Lit. Cant.* 1, pp. 466, 474-6; *Rochester Reg. Hethe* 1, p. 152; 2, p. 1047.

▶ [1 June 1332 Attempted visitation of Exeter chapter. Baker *Chronicon*, p. 50; *Murimuth*, p. 65]

¶ 23 June 1332 Chardstock (Dev.). Mandate reciting that of Itherius de Concoreto for compelling subcollectors to render account for the papal quadrennial tenth. Lincoln Reg. 5, fo. 462r-v.

¶ —1332 Mayfield [month not stated, perhaps Nov. below?]. Constitution declaring all the feasts in the year from which there should be abstention from secular work. Ducarel, fo. 19^r (citing B.L. Cotton MS. Otto A. 15 now lost; Wilkins, *Concilia* 2, p. 560).

¶ 25 June 1332 Mayfield. Mandate reciting letters of Master Thomas de Astley, archdeacon of Middlesex, and Riamon de Mota, commissaries of Itherius de Concoreto requiring execution of letters concerning the tenth. *Bath & Wells Reg. Salopia*, p. 146, no. 572.

¶ 17 July 1332 Mayfield. Mandate to Roger Wyville, bp. of Salisbury, requiring the proper observance of Sundays and a list of named feasts. *Concilia* 2, pp. 560-1.

¶ 23 July 1332 Mortlake. Summons *Sanctorum patrum digesta* for a provincial council to be held at St. Paul's on 4 Sept. Winchester Reg. Stratford, fo. 72^v, edn. no. 694; *Bath & Wells Reg. Salopia*, pp. 103-5, no. 436; *Concilia* 2, p. 561; *Records of Convocation III*, p. 123.

¶ 13 Sept. 1332 Mortlake, with style *apostolice sedis legatus*. Mandate to Bishop Wyville for execution of that of Itherius de Concoreto concerning first fruits. Salisbury Reg. Wyville 1, fo. 12^r: *de mandato exequendo*; *Bath & Wells Reg. Salopia*, p. 108.

¶ 24 Sept. 1332 Mortlake. The abp. appoints John Stratford, bishop of Winchester, as special commissary to carry out the exchange of the benefices of Newington in the exempt jurisdiction of the deanery of Croydon and North Waltham, Winchester docese. *Winchester Reg. Stratfor*d, fo.132^r, edn. no. 1390.

¶ [Oct. 1332—]. The abp. chooses a penitentiary from names submitted by his cathedral priory in a form subsequently objected to by the prior. *Literae Cant.* i, pp. 509-10.

Archbishop Simon Mepham 1328-1333: A Boy Amongst Men

℈ 28 Oct. 1332 Mortlake. Letter to prior and convent of Canterbury affirming the abp.'s right to appoint obedientiaries in accordance with a particular procedure and critising them for not abiding by this, a defect which he declares himself willing to overlook on this occasion. *Literae Cant.* 1, pp. 507-8.

℈ 8 Nov. 1332 Mayfield. Mandate reciting Concoreto's letters re citing of commissaries appointed to collect quadrennial tenth. *Bath & Wells Reg. Salopia*, pp. 128-9, no. 508.

℈ 23 April 1333, Mayfield. Mandate *Iustus et misericors Dominus* (with style *apostolice sedis legatus*) enjoining prayers etc. for the king's victory over the Scots, with fifteen days' indulgence on each performance and encouragement for the diocesan to add his own. Lincoln Reg. Burghersh V, fos. 466r-7r; Winchester Reg. Stratford, fos. 79^v-80^r, edn. no. 772; *Winchester Chart.*, no. 170.

℈ 9 May 1333 Mayfield. Licence for Bp. Wyville to go on pilgrimage abroad, '*sanctorum limina in partibus transmarinis*' (lacking *legatus* in style). Salisbury Reg. Wyville 1, fo. 15^v.

℈ 3 Aug. 1333 Mayfield. Mandate (style *apostolice sedis legatus*) *Ex ore sedentis*, enjoining suffrages for victory against the Scots. Lincoln Reg. Burghersh V, fo. 467^{r-v}; Winchester Reg. Stratford, fo. 85^r, edn. no. 804.

▶ **12 Oct. 1333 Mayfield. Death of Mepham.** *Instrumentum de morte*, subscription of John de Aumberley, notary. CCA DCc Reg. Q, fo. 187r (al. 191).

▶ **22 Oct. 1333.** Laurence Fastolf, canon of St. Paul's on 22nd read out the resignation by John de Wymundham, chaplain, of St. Mary's chantry in St. Andrew's church, Tarring, in the archbishop's immediate jurisdiction, and the letter of John de Montgomery (Monte Gomery), knight, of Goring, the patron, dated 17th from 'La Felde', presenting William de Craneford, chaplain, to Mepham. CCC DCc ChAnt/A219

▶ **26 Oct. 1333 Canterbury. Burial in cathedral.** *Instrumentum de sepultura*, subscription of William de Natyndon, clerk of Canterbury diocese. CCA DCc Reg. Q, fo. 188v (al. 192)

UNDATED OR IMPRECISELY DATED ACTA

¶ —Indulgence conceded for those praying for the soul of the poet, William de Shoreham, vicar of Chart, Kent. Wheeler, 'William de Shoreham', pp. 153-

¶ c. 1328 Mepham requests that following a charter granted in the first parliament of the reign the Barons of the Cinq Ports have accroached on his tenants in parts of Kent to his disinheritance, that of his church and of the king. TNA SC8/97/ 4840.

Mandate at time of 1329 visitation

¶ Summons to the abbot and convent of St. Augustine's Canterbury to appear before him and his auditors of causes in his court on the next juridical day after St. Edward king and martyr (18 March). Thorne, cols. 2039-40.

Appointments of coadjutors during visitation of Salisbury diocese :

¶ Norton (Wilts.). For Henry de Shipton Moyne, vicar of Norton, Salisbury dioc., at his request. Ducarel, fo. 20^r (Reg. Album).

¶ —Nicholas de la Wylie for Masters William de la Wylie, rector of Stalbridge (*Stapelbrigg*), Dors., and Richard de la Wyle, rector of Hawkchurch (*Hanechurche*), Dorset. Ducarel, fos. 20^v 29^r (repeated) (Reg. Album). A Richard de Wylie was instituted to Holy Trnity, Guildford, 23 May 1330. Winchester Reg. Stratford, fo. 118^v, edn. no. 1255.

¶ —M. Ralph de Farnham for William Brutony, rector of Honiton (*Honiton Courtney*), Dors., Ducarel fo. 20v (Reg. Album).

¶ —William de Bremelham, chaplain, for Richard called 'Le Deene', rector of Bremilham, Wilts. Ducarel, fos. 20v-21r (Reg. Album)

Bath & Wells diocese:

¶ Wiveliscombe (Som.). N. de Stoke, chaplain of the chantry of the B.V.M. in Crewkerne church, for William de Bodeston, subdeacon, *cecus et impotens*, having a subdiaconal portion in that church. Ducarel, fo. 21r (Reg. Album).

Institutions in Bath & Wells and Salisbury dioceses:

Bath & Wells

¶ Northover (*Northawe*) (Som.). Of Roger de Berewell, priest, to Northover at presentation of Richard Lovell. Ducarel, fo. 33r (Reg. Album).

¶ Aller (*Kyngesalre*) (Som.). Of John Galenon, priest, presented by John de Clyvedon to the chapel of the B.V.M. there. Ducarel, fo. 30r (Reg. Album).

Salisbury diocese:

¶ Frome Billet (*Frombelt*) (Dors.). Of M. John de Bemenstre, clerk, to Frome, vacant and at his (the abp.'s) presentation. Ducarel, fo. 28r (Reg. Album).

¶ —Of M. Richard de Middleton, clerk, to Askerswell church (*Oskereswell*), Dorset, Salisbury diocese, at the presentation of Agnes, lady of Askerswell. Ducarel, fo. 52v (Reg. Album)

¶ 28 Feb. 1330 Of William de Cornhull to Charlwood by authority of the archbishop's commission [no date and not printed]. *Reg. Martival* 1, p. 407.

Appendix 2

MEPHAM'S CONSTITUTIONS 1329[1]

CONSTITUCIONES PROVINCIALES

Zelari oportet pro domino deo suo ecclesiarum prelatos qui non de sola sunt sua perdicione dampnandi, verum eciam de suis manibus requiret dominus sicut ipse ait sanguinem subditorum adversus eos precipue quos nominis Christiani titulus insignit,[2] et tamen professioni sue dampnatis operibus non desinunt adversari ut quicquid legi divine in corruptis[3] eorum moribus contravenire[4] cognoverint[5] gladio[6] spiritus quod est verbum dei et doctrina salutis interimant[7] et ecclesiastice sarculo discipline veludprovidi cultores extirpent virtutes inserant moresque reforment ut appetitus noxii honestatis debite limitis[8] non excedant, sed inde Christiana professio liberius[9] magis ac magis salutaribus semper proficiat incrementis.

Huius rei gracia nos Symon permissione divina Cant[uariensis] archiepiscopus[10] tocius Anglie primas in nomine sancte[11] Trinitatis, patris[12] filii et spiritus sancti, necessar[ium] fore previdimus[13] auctoritate presentis concilii de fratrum et suffraganeorum nostrorum[14] consensu, ad reformacionem[15] status ecclesiastici in nostra Cant[uariensi] provincia statutis conciliorum prius editis ad ipsorum observacionem[16] penas adicere et quedam eciam nova statuere, quibus vita delinquencium arceatur[17] et salutis profectus uberior inducatur.

Archbishop Simon Mepham 1328-1333: A Boy Amongst Men

De observacione festivitatis diei Parasceves.

Animarum saluti prospicere cupientes, initium ordimur de fontibus salvatoris[18] ut dies illa Sancta Parasceves quo[19] salvator noster dominus Jhesus Christus pro salute omnium[20] preciosam animam suam post multa flagella posuit in cruce, secundum ritum ecclesie in leccione cum silencio, in oracione cum ieiunio, in compunccione cum lacrimis, tran[s]figatur.[21] Auctoritate[22] presentis concilii districcius inhibemus ne de cetero quisquam[23] ipsa die servilibus intendat operibus vel quevis alia excerceat que a pietatis cultu fuerint aliena. Per hoc tamen pauperibus legem non imponimus nec divitibus prohibemus, quin ad agriculturam pauperum promovendam suffragia consueta caritatis intuitu subministrent.

De festivitate Concepcionis Beate Marie celebranda.

Ad hec quia[24] inter omnes sanctos memoria beatissime virginis et matris domini eo frequencius agitur atque festivius quo maiorem graciam apud deum qui eius concepcionem predestinatam ad unigeniti sui temporalem originem et omnium[25] veraciter ordinavit, creditur invenisse, ut per hec salutis nostre quamvis remota primordia in quibus devotis occurrit[26] mentibus spiritualium materia gaudiorum, devocionem omnibus augeat[27] et salutem. Venerabilis Anselmi predecessoris nostri qui post alia quedam ipsius antiquora solemnia concepcionis solenne superaddere dignum duxit vestigiis inherentes statuimus et firmiter precipiendo mandamus quatinus festum Concepcionis predicte in cunctis ecclesiis nostre Cant[uariensis] provincie festive et solenniter de cetero celebretur.

De immunitate bonorum ad ecclesias seu personas
ecclesiasticas pertinencium.

Item, [omnibus *crossed out*] omnes qui de domibus maneriis grangiis aut[28] locis aliis ad archiepiscopos, episcopos, vel alias personas ecclesiasticas seu[29] ad ipsas ecclesias pertinentibus quicquam preter voluntatem aut permissionem dominorum vel eorum qui sunt huiusmodi rerum[30] custodiis deputati abstrahere consumere vel contractare presumpserint abstrahi [fo. 102v] vel[31] consumi vel contractari fecerint seu[32] huiusmodi abstraccionem, consumpcionem aut contraccacionem[33] suo nomine vel a familiaribus suis factam ratam habuerint sacri approbacione huius[34] provincialis concilii pronunciamus et declaramus ecclesiastice libertatis et immunitatis existere violatores et sentenciam excommunicacionis maioris contra huiusmodi violatores in concilio Oxon[iensi] latam incurrere ipso facto.[35] Et ne huiusmodi ecclesiastice immunitatis violatores occasione difficultatis citacionis eorundem evitent sicut hactenus fieri consuevit ne procedi valeat contra ipsos, de fratrum nostrorum et tocius concilii consilio et assensu decernimus quemcumque violatorem huiusmodi si personaliter inveniri et tute adiri valeat personaliter evocand[um], si vero non inveniri vel non tute adiri (*i* interlined above *e*) valeat tunc in domicilio si quod habeat quo tute citari possit, si vero in domicilio quod habet tute citari nequeat tunc in ecclesia cathedrali ipsius domicilii et si nullum habeat vel non constet alium habere domicilium tunc in ecclesia cathedrali loci in quo immunitas ecclesie dicitur esse lesa, et nichilominus in ecclesia parochiali eiusdem loci si tute fieri poterit citacionem decernimus[36] publice faciendam. Huiusmodique citsacionem in domicilio vel in ecclesia ut premittitur publice factam volumus, non solum in casibus supradictis[37] sed eciam in omni casu constitucionis domini Ottoboni quondam apostolice sedis in Anglia legati que incipit *Ad* [*word or part of word crossed out*]*tutela*[38] sit artare[39] [*altered*] citatum, ac si esset citacione personaliter apprehensus et eiusdem quoque[40] citacionis virtute contra ipsum posse procedi ad omnem effectum ad quem posset si citatus personaliter extitisset. Prefatos eciam et quoscumque alios ecclesiastice libertatis seu[41] [*immunitatis crossed out*] violatores decernimus in loco delicti eciam si ibidem non inveniatur[42] posse tam ex officio iudicis quam ad partis instanciam conveniri. Utrum autem huiusmodi violatores ecclesiastice libertatis seu immunitatis inveniri aut[43] tute adiri valeant domicilium ve[44] habeant vel non volumus in dubio stare certificatorium illius cui mandatur citacio facienda et ut in premissis casibus et aliis iniuriam passi iusticiam debitam consequantur districte hoc sacro provinciali concilio approbante precipimus quod omnes iudices ordinarii nostre provincie Cant[uariensis] se invicem sine qualibet difficultate iuvent in citacionibus et execucionibus faciendis ac quibuscumque mandatis licitis exequendis.

De testamentis nativorum non impediendis.

Item, omnes illi qui ascripticiorum vel aliorum servilis condicionis testamenta vel ultimas voluntates quovismodo inpediverint[45] contra consuetudines[46] ecclesie Anglicane hactenus approbatas per excommunicacionis sentenciam compescantur.

De probacionibus testamentorum.

Item, quia[47] locorum ordinarii insinuacionem testamentorum et commissionem administracionis bonorum defunctorum per cautelas exquisitas contra huiusmodi testamentorum executores ut ab eis eo cicius pecuniam extorqueant se ut dicitur reddiderunt hactenus onerosos ordinamus[48] [*interlined above*] quod pro insinuacione[49] testamenti pauperis cuius inventarium bonorum centum solidos sterlingorum non excesserit [vel pro commissione administracionis bonorum huiusmodi executoribus facienda][50] nichil penitus exigatur.

Ut ante sentenciam diffinitivam, non obstante statuto Exoniensi [W Oxoniensis] *possit appellari* 51

Item, quia in consistorio Exon[iensi][52] quoddam statutum dicitur emanasse quo inter cetera prohibetur quod a nullo gravamine iudiciali ante diffinitivam sentenciam appelletur quodque omnes advocati et procuratores eiusdem consistorii ad observacionem huiusmodi statuti astringi debeant vinculo iuramenti, penis eciam aliis in ipso statuto contentis si contra illis[*sic*][53] venerint affligendi.

Nos huiusmodi statutum quod etsi colore verborum superficialiter pallietur, ad auferendum tamen oppressis appellacionis remedium realiter extitit [*part of word cancelled by subpunctuation*] introductum. Et quicquid ex eo vel ob id fuerit subsecutum penitus reprobamus et omnes qui ad observacionem huiusmodi statuti prestiterint iuramentum absolvimus ab eodem.

De impedientibus oblaciones consuetas fieri, et decimas colligere et asportare, absque alicuius doni exaccione.

Item, quia quidam malediccionis filii in nubencium solempniis, mulierum purificacionibus, mortuorum exequiis, et aliis in[54] quibus ipse deus in ministrorum suorum personis solebat oblacionum libamine populariter[55] honorari ad unius denarii vel alterius modice quantitatis oblacionem populi devocionem restringere sunt molliti, residuum oblacionis fidelium suis pro libito[56] vel alienis usibus aliquociens[57] applicantes. Alii vero non attendentes quod[58] deus noster omnipotens cuius est terra et plenitudo eius et universi qui habitant in ea, decimas in signum universalis dominii sibi reddi precepit et pro suo cultu easdem clericis assignavit aliquando maliciose impediunt et impediri ve faciunt seu[59] procurant viros ecclesiasticos ad quos spectat percepcio decimarum eorum ve servitores quominus liberum ingressum et egressum in predia et a prediis de quibus decime huiusmodi proveniunt haberi[60] possunt pro ipsis decimis colligendis custodiendis vel quo voluerint abducendis. Alii eciam nisi prius cirotece vel callige seu quicquam aliud eis dentur vel promittantur decimas huiusmodi asportant aut[61] consumunt asportari consumi ve faciunt seu aliquod dampnum inferunt vel inferri[62] faciunt in eisdem. Alii insuper viros ecclesiasticos ea occasione quod iura ecclesiastica in foro ecclesiastico prosecuntur aut fuerint antea[63] prosecuti maliciose attachiant seu indictant attachiari seu indictari aut alia[64] gravamina inferri faciunt vel procurant. Nos huiusmodi[65] perversorum dampnabilibus consiliis salubre repagulum[66] opponere cupientes nichil novum statuentes set antiquorum canonum sanctita[67] in medium deducantes, universos et singulos huiusmodi instigatores,[68] inpeditores aut[69] alios supradictos per quorum nephandas machinaciones ecclesiis vel[70] [fo. 103r] ipsarum rectoribus, vicariis ac ministris[71] quicquam dampni infertur vel[72] subtrahitur honoris aut[73] comodi consueti presentis declaracione concilii pronunciamus universos et singulos in premissis vel eorum aliquo in posterum delinquentes vinculo excommunicacionis involvi, reservata loci diocesano absolucione eorum preterquam in mortis articulo, quousque ipsorum ministerio in contrarium laborante ecclesiis fuerit popularis devocio efficaciter restituta ac viris ecclesiasticis sic lesis de huiusmodi excessibus plenarie satisfactum.[74]

De matrimonio non solemnizando absque bannorum edicione.

Item, quia ex contractibus matrimonialibus absque bannorum edicione prehabita initis nonnulla pericula provenerunt[75] et manifestum est in dies provenire, omnibus et singulis suffraganeis nostris precipimus statuendo quod decretalem *Cum inhibicio,*[76] qua prohibetur ne qui matrimonium contrahant bannis non premissis in singulis ecclesiis parochialibus sue diocesis pluribus diebus solempnibus cum maior aderit populi[77] multitudo exponi faciant in wlgari ipsamque faciant firmiter observari, penam[78] quibusvis sacerdotibus eciam non parochialibus[79] qui contractibus matrimonialibus ante solempnem edicionem bannorum initis presumpserit interesse penam suspensionis ab officio per triennium infligendo, et huiusmodi contrahentes eciam si nullum subsit impedimentum pena debita percellendo. Quivis[80] eciam sacerdos sive secularis sive regularis extiterit qui solempnizacioni matrimonii extra ecclesiam parochialem[81] absque episcopi loci diocesani speciali licencia celebrate[*sic*][82] presumpserit[83] interesse ipso facto[84] per annum integrum ab officio sit suspensus.[85]

De defectibus domorum ad beneficia ecclesiastica spectancium reparandis.

Item, statuimus quod nulla inquisicio super defectibus domorum aut[86] aliorum ad beneficium ecclesiasticum spectancium de cetero facienda valeat in alterius preiudicium nisi fiat per viros fidedignos in forma iuris iuratos, ipso ad hoc primitus evocato[87] integram vero estimacionem defectuum in domibus aut aliis ad beneficium ecclesiasticum spectantibus repertorum sive per inquisicionem sive per viam composicionis[88] facta extiterit loci diocesanus in reparacionem ipsorum defetuum converti faciat infra competentem terminum ipsius arbitrio moderandum.

ENDNOTES

[1] A transcription of the copy in the register of Bishop Northburgh (Lichfield Joint Record Office B/A/1/3 fos. 102r-103r) collated with Lyndwood 'Lynd' and Wilkins 'W'. No notice has been taken of orthographical differences or of minor changes in word order. Wilkins used BL Cotton MS Otho A 15 (*recte* 16, lost) and collated it with Lambeth MS 17 (L), now MS 538; Ely MS 235 (E) now Cambridge University Library Gg vi 21; and Bodleian Library MS Digby 81 (B). Lambeth MS. 538 has now been used as the basis for the text of the constitutions appearing in *Records of Convocation III*, pp. 110-14. The most important of the somewhat slight variants I have footnoted with the same sigla. The rubrics are those of Wilkins but with orthography to accord with that of the text. The principal variations noted by Wilkins in L, E, B are in the rubrics. These are not footnoted below. The Queen's College, Oxford, MS. LIV (late 15th cent.), formerly belonging to Sir Robert Cotton, contains Mepham's statutes at fos. 406v-408r, followed by a section *De consuetudinibus observandis una cum statutis predictis et de pena non servantium ipsa statuta*. I am grateful for information provided by Helen Powell, at the time assistant librarian. D. M. Owen, *The Medieval Canon Law* (Cambridge 1990), p. 39, using MS. LIV, attributes 'statutes for the Court of Arches' to Mepham. In fact the MS. contains the provincial statutes of Winchelsey (attributed), Stratford and Mepham and following the first some unwritten customs (*In primis si pars appellans*) for the Arches (392v). At fo. 393v are constitutions (*Cum ad curie nostre*) for the Court attributed to Abp. John [Stratford] (dated from Lambeth 30 July 1320!). See H.O. Coxe, *Catalogus codicum in Collegiis Aulisque Oxoniensibus* (Oxford 1852), pp. 8-9. Cheney, *Statutes and Synods II*, p. 496 n. 3, remarks that a sentence in the Statutes of York (1241X1255) is attributed to Mepham in Trinity Coll. Dublin, MS. B. 5. 3.

[2] Lynd, W *insignivit*.

[3] Lynd, W lack *in*.

[4] Lynd, W *contraire*.

[5] Lynd adds *qui*.

[6] L, B add *sancti*.

7. W *doctrina salutis nocentes vitiorum silices non modo interimant.* Lynd as W but lacking *modo.*
8. Lynd, W *limites.*
9. W *libentius.* L *magis ac magis, libentiusque.*
10. Lynd adds *et.*
11. Lynd, W add *et individuae.*
12. W adds *et.*
13. W omits *previdimus.*but adds after *fore: duximus statuendum.*
14. Lynd omits *nostrorum.*
15. Lynd *confirmationem.*
16. Lynd *conservacionem.*
17. W *arceantur.*
18. Lynd, W *statuimus itaque et ordinamus.*
19. Lynd, W *qua.*
20. Lynd, W *hominum.*
21. Lynd, W *lachrymis festive celebretur.*
22. Lynd adds *etiam.*
23. Lynd, W *quispiam.*
24. W *Adhoc quod.*
25. Lynd, W add *salutem.*
26. W *occurritur.*
27. Lynd, W *in omnibus augeant.*
28. W *et.*
29. W *et.*
30. W omits this word.
31. W omits.
32. W *vel.* L, E have *rei custodes de praesenti abstrahere.*
33. W *contrectationem.*
34. W *hujusmodi.*
35. *Councils & Synods II,* p. 106, Council of Oxford (1222), c. 1.

36 W adds *fore*.

37 W *praedictis*.

38 *Councils & Synods II,* pp. 762-4 Legatine Council of London (1268), c. 12.

39 W *arctare*.

40 W *ejusdemque*.

41 W *vel*.

42 W *inveniantur*.

43 W *ac*.

44 W *ne*; Lynd. *et utrum domicilium habeant vel non*.

45 Lynd, W *impedierint*.

46 Lynd, W *consuetudinem*.

47 W *qui*.

48 W *statuimus*.

49 W *et approbatione*.

50 Phrase omitted but present in Lynd, W.

51 *Records of Convocation III*, p. 112 has a note (393) to the effect that no such canon appears among those of the Council of Oxford (1222).

52 Lynd, W, *concilio Oxoniensi,* but inconsistently *consistorii* lower down. E has *consistorio*.

53 Lynd, *id* ; W *illud*.

54 Lynd, W omit *in*.

55 L, E *specialiter*.

56 W *suis libitis*.

57 Lynd, W *multoties*.

58 Lynd, W add *dominus*.

59 Lynd, W *vel*.

60 Lynd, W. *habere*.

61 W *et*.

62 Lynd, W *inferrive*.

63 Lynd, W *vel ante ea fuerint*.

64. W *attachiant, indictant, vel judicant, attachiari, indictari, judicarive aut eis alia.* Lynd likewise, but with *indicant* for *judicant*.
65. Lynd, W *igitur.*
66. W *remedium* but with *repagulum* in the collated Bodleian Lib. MS Digby 81.
67. Lynd *sancita;* W *statuta.*
68. Lynd, W add *et.*
69. Lynd, W *et.*
70. Lynd, W *aut.*
71. Lynd *seu vicariis aut ministris.* W *vel vicariis aut ministris.*
72. Lynd, W. *aut.*
73. Lynd, W *et.*
74. Lynd adds a paragraph here with references to canon law beginning *Nota quod rector habens parochianum suspectum timens se posse in decimus defraudari,* ending *de questione hujus modi.*
75. Lynd *perveniunt.* W *proveniunt.*
76. *Extra* 4, 3, c. 3. L, W add *Extra de clandestin' desponsal.*
77. Lynd, W *major populi affuerit.*
78. Lynd, W omit. The word is not necessary since it occurs below.
79. Lynd, W *etiam parochialibus vel non parochialibus.*
80. Lynd *omnis.*
81. Lynd, W add *vel capellam habentem jura parochialia ab antiquo.*
82. W *celebrare.* Lynd *solennizationem matrimonii extra ecclesiam, vel capellam habentem jura parochialia ab antiquo, absque episcopi loci dioecesani speciali licentia celebrare presumpserit.*
83. Lynd, W add *aut.*
84. Lynd, W *eo ipso.*
85. Lynd adds a comment: *Nec credo quod episcopus potest dispensare infra annum* and cites the canon law references.
86. Lynd, W *vel.*
87. Lynd, W *ipsis ad hoc primitus vocatis qui ab hoc laedi poterint.*
88. W adds *ipsa.*

Appendix 3

Convocations, Provincial Councils and Other Ecclesiastical Assemblies

Type of assembly	Date, place and purpose	Outcome & grants	Abp.'s mandates	Royal Writs	References
1. Provincial Council	27 Jan. 1329 St. Paul's, London Concerning a grant and other matters touching the state of church, clergy & people, correction of excesses, reformation of manners (*morum*)	Refused grant. Could scarcely support papal burdens. Laity had granted sufficient subsidy Provincial Constitutions *Zelari oportet* issued (*edite*) *RC III*, 110-14 Murderers of Bp. Stapeldon excommunicated	29 Nov. 1328 Mayfield	None, but Parliament adjourned from Salisbury met 9 Feb. at Westminster	Winchester Reg. Stratford, fo. 43[r] edn. no. 441 *Concilia* ii, 548-54 *RC III*, 110-14

Archbishop Simon Mepham 1328-1333: A Boy Amongst Men

Type of assembly	Date, place and purpose	Outcome & grants	Abp.'s mandates	Royal Writs	References
2. Convocation	**11 March 1330** Winchester Cathedral. To treat about urgent business of English church and realm to be considered at length in parliament [same date] Mepham not present at latter acc. to royal writ of 18 March [below].		11 Feb. 1330 Mortlake	Eltham 27 Feb. Order for parliament to assemble 12 March re France, Aquitaine and the 'crusade'. No action by clergy on subsidy owing to Abp.'s absence	Lincoln Reg. Burghersh 5, fos. 403r-v; 429r-v; *Concilia* 2, 557-8 *RC III*, 115-17
3. Convocation	**16 April 1330** Lambeth manor To discuss matters raised at Winchester parliament, including subsidy for king. *Locum tenens* of Abp. acted according to chronicler Dene	Grant refused Bp. Hethe allegedly ringleader	24 March 1330 Mortlake	18 March 1330 Winchester 15 April 1330 Woodstock	Lincoln Reg. Burghersh 5, fo. 429r-v [Bp. summons his clergy to Northampton for 12 April] HR, fo. 56r; *Concilia* 2, 558-9 *RC III*, 117-22

~ 115 ~

Type of assembly	Date, place and purpose	Outcome & grants	Abp.'s mandates	Royal Writs	References
4. Provincial Council	4 Sept. 1332 St. Paul's, London Wrangle over summons in view of Abp.'s attempt to rally support against Bp. Grandisson. Appeals launched against Abp. under leadership of Orleton. Only Rochester and Salisbury demurred, but Stratford was absent on royal business.		23 July 1332 Mortlake	None	Winchester Reg. Stratford, fo. 72ᵛ, edn nos. 694-6; HR, fo. 63r; *Bath & Wells Reg. Salopia*, 183-5; *Concilia* 2, 561 *RC III*, 123-7

Appendix 4

Extracts from Canterbury Register Q

Canterbury Cathedral Archives DCc Register Q, fo. 126ʳ.

Queen Isabella urges Mepham's promotion.

Littera domine Isabelle regine Anglie domino pape directa pro negocio elecionis et electi. Venerabili in Christo patri &c. Variis tribulacionum angustiis a multis retro temporibus in rebus quam personis que plaga communi afflicta Anglie regni maiores et minores inter bellorum discrimina e quibus premissa provenerunt ob quorundam prelatorum regni eiusdem incuriam et regimen indiscretum ut verisimiliter opinamur non inmerito formidant pacem internam affectantes quam prosequi speramus indubie si ecclesie Cant' de p[astore] deo grato et populo dicti regni acceptabili provideri contingat. Ipsa enim quasi[?] mater filiarum fecunda multarum regimini presidet que Angl[ie] maiorem partem et ... Walliam lacte fidei refossilat et eas quasi humiles maternarum viarum sectatrices quo voluerit dirigit et adducit quas cum per pacis viam reduxerit toti regno predicto pax preparatur. Sane pater reverende ... prior et conventus ecclesie Christi ad quos de pastoris electo noscitur pertinere excellentis probitatis virum magister Simonem de Mepham sacre theologie professorem in ecclesie predicte archiepiscopum novum[?] spiritus sancti gracia ut firmiter creditur concorditer elegerunt qui personaliter ad sacrosanctam sedem apostolicam eleccionis sue negocium probaturum iam dudum accessit cui cor nostrum ac populi regni predicti adhesit in tantum quod si sub eius umbra presidentis in ecclesia predicta memorata protegi valeamus quietis et pacis nos credimus nostris temporibus debere perpetua iocunditate letari. Vestram igitur paternitatem . . . ex nostra deliberacione sed ex predicti populi frequenti et felice corde sincero preces effundimus cordiales scientes quod idem negocium nostrum et tocius populi provincie Cantuariensis reputamus commune et in unum convenients, alii proceres regni et nos vobis duxerimus sub hac stili serie singuli conscribend'. Intelligentes pro certo quod alterius quam electi predicti prefeccio in ecclesia memorata in populo scandalum . . . et scisma quod absit diucius duratur'.

Ibid., fo. 127v. *Mepham's confirmation and consecration.*
De confirmacione S[imonis] archiepiscopi

Et memorandum quod xxvii die Maii, videlicet vito kalendarum Junii, anno domino MoCCCmoXXVIII [interlined and unreadable owing to binding] presentibus cardinalibus in publico consistorio dominus Johannes papa xxiius predictam eleccionem [et?] electum Cantuar' sollempniter confirmavit. Et die dominica in octabis Trinitatis videlicet quinto die mensis Junii [anno predicto interlined] fuit dictus electus consecratus a domino Petro Episcopo Penestrino Cardinali de speciali mandato domini pape in ecclesia fratrum Predicatorum Avinion'. Et postea quarto die sequenti palleum videlicet plenitudinem pontificalis officii de corpore Beati Petri sumptum recepit anno domini MoCCCmoXXVIIIo.

Ibid. fo. 129r-v. *Copy of a notarial instrument attesting the commission, dated 19 June 1328, appointing Master Edmund de Mepham, the archbishop's brother, as Official or*

Archbishop Simon Mepham 1328-1333: A Boy Amongst Men

vicar general within the diocese and province. Subsequently the archbishop takes ship from Antwerp to Dover, and then travels via Chartham and Rochester to Gravesend where he crosses the Thames.

Commissio magistri E[dmundi] de Mepham generalis vicarii S[imonis] archiepiscopi.

In crastino [8 July 1328?] magister Edmundus de Mepham domini... archiepiscopi vicarius generalis publicavit coram ... priore commissionem suam, cuius tenor talis erat.

Simon permissione divina Cantuar' archiepiscopus tocius Anglie primas venerabili et discreto viro magistro Edmundo de Mepham canonico Landaven[si] sacre pagine doctori, germano nostro, salutem in domino sempiternam. Ex iniuncti officii debito provocamur quinimmo quadam urgentis consciencie neccessitate compellimur ut circa execucionem impositi oneris, cui personali ministerio sic cito nequivimus intendere, tales habeamus personas quarum cura et providencia defectus, qui possent ex nostra provenire absencia, prout est possibile supleantur, et que reformacione indigent reformentur omnibusque exhibeatur iusticie complementum. Proinde attendentes quod divino assistente presidio vos de cuius providencia et discrecione probabiliter nobis constat partem iniuncti nobis oneris comode poteritis supportare, quodque clero et populo civitatis diocesis et provincie Cantuar' eritis [? Difficult to read] non modicum fructuosi, usque ad nostre voluntatis beneplacitum in spiritualibus ac eciam in quantum nobis licet in temporalibus, tenore presencium vos facimus [fo. 129v] et ordinamus nostrum officialem seu vicarium generalem, vobis expressius committentes atque mandantes ut omnes causas tam spirituales quam civiles, seu criminales, ad nostrum forum et curiam spectantes, audire cognoscere examinare, ac eciam diffinire, ipsasque per vos, vel alium seu alios, possitis et debeatis execucioni debite demandare. Ecclesias autem prebendas atque beneficia que in civitate diocesi et provincia predictis quovismodo vacaverint imposterum, vel hactenus vacaverint, quorum ad nos collacio seu confirmacio noscitur pertinere nostre collacioni et confirmacioni totaliter reservamus. In quorum omnium testimonium, presentes litteras nostras in forma publica fieri fecimus per notarium et scribam nostrum infrascriptum, nostrique sigilli munimine roborari. Dat' et act' Avinioni in domo habitacionis nostre, anno nativitatis domini MoCCCmoXXVIIIo secundum cursum sacrosancte Romane ecclesie, indiccione undecima, mensis Junii die xixa, pontificatus sanctissimi patris in Christo et domini, domini Johannis divina providencia pape xxiidi anno xiimo, et consecracionis nostre primo. Presentibus domino Thoma de Woghope presbitero, Roberto Viannde et Godefrido Hunstane litteratis, testibus ad premissa vocatis specialiter et rogatis.

Et ego Simon de Cherringg' clericus Cant' diocesis, publicus apostolica auctoritate notarius, prefatis faccioni et ordinacioni omnibusque aliis et singulis prout suprascribuntur interfui una cum testibus prescriptis, et ea sic fieri vidi et audivi, et presentes de rogatu et mandato prefati reverendi in Christo patris domini Simonis archiepiscopi in hanc publicam formam redegi anno, indiccione, mense, die et loco prefatis, meumque signum apposui consuetum.

Expeditis omnibus negociis eleccionis et electi in Curia Romana archiepiscopus de curia recessit, et per Campaniam et Hanoniam venit apud Antwerp in Brabancia, et ibidem navem ascendit. Et die Sancti Bertini videlicet quinto die Septembris apud Dovor' applicuit. Deinde per Chertham et Roff' usque Gravesende iter direxit. Et ibidem Tamisiam transivit versus dominum regem qui tunc erat in partibus Lincoln' dirigens gressus suos.

Ibid. fo. 130r (cxv). See also TNA SC6/1128/7-9. The roll 1128/7 lists lands of the see of Canterbury in Croydon bailiwick released by the keepers of the temporalities, as well as the chapel ornaments and jewels said to be in the custody of John de la Chaumbre, the archbishop's clerk.

Ecclesiastical ornaments released on 8 September 1328 to the chapel of Archbishop Simon Mepham

[Rubric]

Ornamenta ecclesiastica liberat[a] ad capellam domini S[imonis] Archiepiscopi.

¶ Ornamenta ecclesiastica subscripta in duabus cistis rubeis amalatis liberata fuerunt ad capellam venerabilis patris domini Simonis dei gracia Cant' archiepiscopi tocius Anglie primatis die Nativitatis beate Marie, anno domini MoCCCmo XXVIIIo [8 Sept. 1328], per indenturam factam inter dominum Hugonem de Sancta Margareta tunc sacristam ecclesie Christi Cantuar' et dominum Thomam de Woghope custodem capelle dicti patris videlicet:

¶ Crux portatil[is] argentea.

¶ Item, mitra domini Johannis [Pecham] archiepiscopi.

¶ Item, baculus eiusdem argent[eus] et operat[us].

¶ Item, cirothecc domini R[oberti] de Wynchelese archiepiscopi cum perulis et gemmis in platis quadrat[is] et magnis tassellis rotund[is].

¶ Item, anulus pontificalis magnus cum saphiro oblongo et quatuor pramis cum quatuor margaritis.

¶ Item, tres acus aurei ad palleum quilibet cum uno rubino baleys et. ii. smaragdinis et. ii. saphiris.

¶ Item, ii. sandalia cum galochis de rubeo samicto brudat[a] armis regis Anglie.

¶ Item, calix. i. cum patena argent[ea] et deaurat[a] intus et extra cum nodo in medio cum perulis et gemmis operatis ponder[is] xlii s.

¶ Item, ii. urcioli argent[ei] unde. i. deaurat[us] et alius amalat[us] ponder[is] xxii s.

¶ Item, ii. candelabr[a] argent[ea] cum tribus pedibus argent[eis] domini R[oberti] archiepiscopi predicti.

¶ Item, thurribulum argent[eum] et deaurat[um] ponder[is] lxxiii s. iiii d.

¶ Item, vas ad thus cum coclear[e] argent[eo] ponderis xxii s.

¶ Item, vas argent[eus] ad aquam benedictam ponderis lxxiii s. iiiid.

¶ Item, aspersor[ium] argent[eum] ponder[is] xiii s. iiii d.

- ⁊ Item, pixis eburnea ad oblat[a].
- ⁊ Item, crismator[ium] argent[eum] domini Walteri [Reynolds] archiepiscopi.
- ⁊ Item, capa chori. i. }
- ⁊ casula. i.} pro domino archiepiscopo
- ⁊ Tunica et dalmatica.
- ⁊ Item, tunica et dalmatica pro diacono et subdiacono de rubeo samicto brudat[e] cum arboribus aureis et cum aurifrigio de perulis et avibus operatis. [fo. 130v]
- ⁊ Item. ii. cape de rubeo samicto cum. ii. tassellis aureis pro. ii. clericis capelle.
- ⁊ Item, alba. i. cum amictu et cingulo brudat[a] cum coronacione beate Marie ex parte una et matre et filio ex parte altera pro domino . . . archiepiscopo.
- ⁊ Item, stola et manipulum cum scutis consut[i] et brudat[i]'.
- ⁊ Item, corporalia brudat[a] cum crucifixo et coronacione beate Marie.
- ⁊ Item, ii. albe cum amictibus pro diacono et subdiacono de serico consut[is].
- ⁊ Item, stola. i. et duo manipuli pro diacono et subdiacono brudat[i].
- ⁊ Item, palla altaris cum frontell[o] de scutis brudat[o].
- ⁊ Item, palla. i. sine frontell[o].
- ⁊ Item, manutergium. i. ad manus.
- ⁊ Item, pannus. i. ad sacrarium.
- ⁊ Item, campana. i. ad summar' capelle.
- ⁊ Item equ[u]s. i. summar[ius] cum tapeto et barehid[o] et alio harnas[io] pertinent[ibus] precii x librarum.
- ⁊ Item, magnus liber qui dicitur pontificale domini Johannis [Pecham] archiepiscopi.
- ⁊ Item, biblia domini R[oberti Winchelsey] archiepiscopi supradicti,

Ibid. fo. 130v Mayfield 30 November 1328. *Mepham appoints Brother Peter, bishop of Corbavia, to ordain in Christ Church Canterbury on Saturday in Embertide next (17 December) both those monks presented by the precentor, and beneficed clerks* *of the city, diocese, or immediate jurisdictions presented by the commissary general with the assistance of the official of the archdeacon of Canterbury.*

Commissio domini Petri episcopi Corbav' de ordinibus celebrandis in ecclesia Cantuar' sede plena.

Simon permissione divina Cant' archiepiscopus et cetera, venerabili fratri domino Petro dei gracia episcopo Corbav', salutem et fraternam in domino caritatem. Ad celebrandum ordines vice nostra in instanti die sabbati quatuor temporum post festum Sancte Lucie virginis prox[ime] futur[um] in ecclesia nostra Christi Cantuar' et per manuum vestrarum imposicionem ordinandum personas religiosas quas . . . precentor ecclesie nostre predicte, necnon alias personas ecclesiastica beneficia optinentes in nostris civitate diocesi et iurisdiccionibus immediatis quas dilectus nobis in Christo magister Thomas commissarius noster Cant' generalis assistente sibi officialis . . . archidiaconi nostri Cant', vobis duxerint presentandas, dum tamen huiusmodi ordinandis aliquod canonicum non obsistat, vobis tenore presencium committimus potestatem. In cuius rei testimonium sigillum nostrum presentibus duximus apponendum. Dat' apud Maghefeld' ii kalen' Decembris anno domini MoCCCmoXXVIII et consecracionis nostre primo.

Appendix 5

OTHER ORIGINAL DOCUMENTS

NOTE ON THE ARCHBISHOP'S COURT BOOKS. CCA ChAnt/A/36/i (1325-29), ChAnt/A/36/ii (1328-30).

The first of these is of 18 folios comprising the period December 1325 to July 1326 in Abp. Reynolds's time; December 1327 to June 1328 during the following vacancy, Reynolds having died on 16 November; and July 1328 to April 1329—the early part of Mepham's archiepiscopate. The first entry (fo. 1r) is dated 19 December 1325. This folio has been much damaged, a fate that to a greater or lesser extent has befallen the whole manuscript. The last session (fo. 17/18r), of 8 April 1329, was conducted in Bishopsbourne church by the auditors Masters Laurence Fastolf and Robert de Weston. The foliation (top right) is modern but fo. 10 is repeated. Subsequently the correct numbers 11-18 were added at the base. I have used *recto* and *verso* to locate entries.

The later cover has a fairly recent title: PROCEEDINGS BEFORE MASTER ROBERT RIDDESWELL AND ROBERT DE WESTON. Other auditors who acted were Masters Richard de Haut, John de Badesley, and on the last folio Thomas de Canterbury, described as the archbishop's special commissary. Although Mepham was elected 11 December 1327 and consecrated 5 June in

Archbishop Simon Mepham 1328-1333: A Boy Amongst Men

the following year the first specific mention of him as archbishop is on fo. 17r at a session of 8 July 1328 when M. Robert de Weston is designated his auditor-general. On the *verso* of this folio under the date 26 July Weston is said to be acting while Mepham—given his proper title at this point—is *in remotis*. On fo. 15v a session of the court opened on 17 May 1328 before M. Robert in Christ Church, Canterbury, *sede vacante*, whilst fos. 16r and 16v record entries, of 3 and 25 June 1328 respectively, which are similarly described. This was because news of papal approval and of Mepham's consecration at the Curia would have taken some time to reach Canterbury. As shown in Chapter 2, he himself only arrived back in the first week of September.

The second manuscript is partially paginated in a modern hand, but somewhat erratically. For convenience of reference I have renumbered it 1-42 and as in the earlier manuscript have worked from digital images provided from the Canterbury archives. The first page is badly faded and partially indecipherable but the opening rubric commences: *Registrum actorm coram reverendo patre domino Symone [archiepiscopo]*. It records the cases in the archbishop's audience court between the years 1328 and 1330. The first visibly dated entry is on the second page, that of 26 October *ut supra* [1328], the final entry is dated 26 July 1330. The manuscript has the appearance of a rough draft in that some entries are crossed out, others crowded in or left unfinished, while interlineations abound. Spaces were frequently left for subsequent procedure and the auditors are often merely given their surnames. As is common in court books the regular phrases are highly abbreviated. The cases are both *ex officio*, that is moved on behalf of the archbishop in his judicial capacity, and *ex parte* brought by some other party or parties.

The location of the court varied considerably. Sessions took place in chapels or or other venues within the archbshop's manors, such as Charing, Harrow, Otford, Mayfield, Slindon, and more particularly Mortlake. Most sessions were held in parish churches such as St. Alphege in Canterbury, Charing, Chartham, Croydon, Lambeth, Maidstone, Mayfield, Teynham, Trottiscliffe, Wingham, and Wrotham. In one instance, on 22nd July 1329, the court was held in Horton church by Windsor, in Lincoln diocese. Occasionally use was made of a cemetery or porch rather than the church itself. Monastic churches were used on two occasions: Leeds, a house of Augustinian canons, and Malling, one of Benedictine nuns.

As has been shown in chapter 2 above, the chancellor M. Thomas de Hockley whose name, without the evidence of the court book, might have remained unknown, was active in his role as principal auditor, assisted principally by M. Robert de Weston The archbishop only appears once in person and that was on the occasion of an appointment of a proctor, as will appear in the extract below from p. 42 of the court book.

EXTRACTS:

Papal bull of privilege

Avignon 14 July 1328. *Bull of Pope John XXII granting the archbishop's petition that while in places and manors in which he happened to be staying he should not be compelled to respond to mandates from the apostolic see or its officials demanding his response in various places under penalty of excommunication, suspension or interdict.*

CCA DCc ChAnt/A/36/ii, p. 4 [Reg. Aven. 31, fo. 122v].

Johannes episcopus servus servorum Dei venerabili fratri Symoni archiepiscopo Cant', salutem et apostolicam benediccionem. Clara tue devocionis merita et affectus quem ad nos et Romanam ecclesiam geris provertentur [? MS unclear] ut illa tibi favore benivolo concedimus per que status tuus tranquille pacis munimen fulciatur. Sane sicut peticio tua nobis nuper exhibita continebat frequenter contingit quod per sedem apostolicam necnon officiales vel auditores delegatos seu subdelegatos sedis eiusdem committuntur diversa negocia et execuciones eorum archiepiscopo Cantuar' qui est pro tempore cum adieccione penarum excommunicacionis suspensionis et interdicti nisi fecerit quod mandatur quorum execuciones interdum extra loca seu maneria ubi dictus archiepiscopus moratur in diversis locis fieri exiguntur ad que prefatum archiepiscopum qui est pro tempore propter statum honorabilem quem ipse in ecclesia et provincia suis tenet non deteret accedere nec ipse posset absque incomodo et gravi onere expensarum ac nichilominus illi qui huiusmodi negocia prosequentur nec eidem archiepiscopo nec aliis quos idem archiepiscopus vult mittere ad execucionem predictam proficiscentibus extra suas ecclesias seu domicilia nolunt satisfacere de expensis et interdum nisi archiepiscopus suis sumptibus proficiscatur ad huiusmodi negocia exequenda dicunt eundem predictas sentencias incurreret et ipsum[?] faciunt predictis ligatum sentenciis nunciari ex quibus in partibus illis quandoque magna scandala oriuntur. Quare nobis humiliter supplicasti ut providere tibi et statui tuo super hoc de oportuno remedio dignaremur. Nos igitur huiusmodi tuis supplicacionibus inclinati ut ad huiusmodi execuciones [not fully readable] tibi per litteras apostolicas committendas personaliter faciendas extra loca vel maneria tua in quibus [?] talia mandata recipere te contigerit minime usque ad apostolice sedis beneplacitum tenearis nullas [? MS obscure] per alium seu alios valeas explicare nec ad id compelli possis invitus auctoritate tibi presencium indulgemus. Nulli ergo omnino homini liceat hanc paginam nostre concessionis infringere vel ea ausu temeraria contraire. Si quis autem hoc attempare presumpserit indignacionem omnipotentis Dei et beatorum Petri et Pauli apostolorum eius se noverit incursum. Dat' Avinon' ii Id' Julii pontificatus nostri anno duodecimo.

5 April 1329, *St. Alphege's church, Canterbury. 'Acta' of the archbishop's commissaries— Thomas de Hockeley, chancellor, Laurence Fastolf, and Robert de Weston—with respect to comperta arising from visitation of the city and diocese of Canterbury.*

CCA D Cc ChAnt/A/36/ii, p. 6

Acta coram nobis Thoma de Hokkel' venerabilis domini patris. S. &c. cancellario et magistris Laurencio Fastolf et Roberto de Weston dicti patris in omnibus causis et correccionum negociis visitacionem ['per' crossed out] eiusdem patris suarum civitatis et diocesis qualitercumque contingentibus commissariis generalibus et ipsis curie causarum et negociorum auditoribus in ecclesia Sancti

Elphegi Cant' quinto die mensis Aprilis anno domini millesimo ccc^{mo}xxix. Cum constaret nobis religiosos viros abbatem et conventum de Langedon Cant' diocesis ordinis Premonstratensis dictos diem et locum ex assignacione habuisse ad exhibendum et ostendendum eorum ius et munimenta super appropriacionibus ecclesiarum quas in proprios usus optinere pretendebant in diocesi supradicto ipsisque religiosis per fratrem Henricum de Byoolte canonicum de Langedon comparentibus et domino Johanne Malemayns milite per Stephanum de Elham procuratorem suum similiter comparente. Asseruit idem procurator principalis interesse domini sui predicti admitti ad assistendum allegandum et proponendum pro iure suo in negocio quod iustum erit in negocio exhibicionis munimentorum quatenus concernere poterat ecclesiam de Waldwarschar' [Waldershare] dicte diocesis ipsis religiosis ut dicitur appropriatam, propositoque per partem dicti militis quodam articulo super negocium [?] suum in quo petebatur se sub certa forma admitti ad faciendum in dicto articulo et ulterius in hoc negocio quod iustum erit. Diem crastinum videlicet vi die Aprilis loco quo prius partibus prefigimus et assignamus. Quo die partibus comparentibus ut prius prefixus est eis dies proximus iuridicus post Quasimodo geniti ubicumque &c ad faciendum quod prius.

Undated. '*Ex officio' case against Hugh de Hasstheland, tailor of London, and Roger Makepays, bailiff of the king's Marshalsea prison, for attaching the rector of Kingsdon in his rectory and taking him to the Marshalsea in London on account of a debt to the said Hugh.*

CCA DCc ChAnt/A/36/ii, p. 5

In causa rectoris de Kyngesdonne ex officio mota contra Hugonem de Hasstheland de London' cissorem et Rogerum Makepays ballivum Mareschallar' domini regis, ipsis Hugone et Rogero personaliter comparentibus, confessatoque per dictum Rogerum quod dictum rectorem in rectoria sua predicta attachiavit tanquam ballivus regis, et auctoritate regis ipsum duxit London' ubi in Marescall' domini regis detinebatur propter debitum in quo predicto Hugone tenebatur, et iurato de stando mandatis ecclesie iniunctum sibi fuit per dominum quod sexies ad beatum Thomam Cant' de loco ubi delictum commisit eat et offerat in singulis vicibus i cereum ponderis ii libras cere.

Mortlake 28 December [1329]. *Memorandum of the receipt by M. William de Fysshebourne of a letter of obligation for the payment of £40 borrowed by the archbishop from the bishop of Chichester [John Langton], to be delivered to the bishop by the hand of the said William on the feast of St. Dunstan [19 May 1330] following.*

CCA DCc ChAnt/A/36/ii, p. 8

Memorandum quod v^m [quintum] kalen[darum] Januarii anno domini supradicto sub data apud Mourtelak magister Willelmus de Fysshebourne recepit i literam obligatoriam de quadraginta libris, a domino Cicestrensi episcopo per dominum Cant' mutuat[is], solvend[is] eidem in festo Sancti Dunstani datam predictam proximo sequenti eidem [repeated *sic*] episcopo per dictum magistrum Willelmum liberandam. Et fuit sigillata magno sigillo.

[**Crossed out**] *Memorandum that Robert Leueye, executor of the testament of E[dmund] de Mepham, sought an account from John Flemyng of the goods which he received with respect to the will of Symon de Faversham, whose executor M. E[dmund] had been. John admitted that he had received one cup worth 15s. and another three which he restored to M. E[dmund].*

CCA DCc ChAnt/A/36/ii, p. 8 (base)

⁋ Memorandum quod Robertus Leueye executor testamenti Magistri E. de Mepham petiit compotum reddi a domino Johanne Flemyng' de bonis per eum receptis contingentibus testamentum magistri Symonis de Faversham cuius executor Magister E. predictus extiterat. Decretum est quod idem dominus

Johannes personaliter comparens veniat plene instructus ad compotum reddendum de receptis suis de bonis predictis ad secundum Magdalene.

¶ Et memorandum quod idem Johannes fatetur se recepisse unum coopertorium precii xv solidorum et habuisse alia tria coopertoria que restituit eodem magistro E.

'Ex officio' case against the prior of Horton, who had not rendered obedience for the church of Brabourne, Kent, which was ill-roofed, and failed to greet the archbishop with a peal of bells on his arrival at the priory.

CCA DCc ChAnt/A/36/ii, p. 9

¶ In negocio ex officio contra priorem de Hortone pro eo quod non fecit obedienciam pro ecclesia de Brabourn quando ad id vocari fuit. Habet iii^m diem juridicum post festum Sancti Dunstani

¶ Item non pulsavit contra archiepiscopum venientem iuxta portam de Horton. Habet diem ad tercium Dunstani ad fac[iendum]

¶ Item cancellus de Brabourn est male coopertus. Et idem tenet ecclesiam illam appropriatam et plura sunt capitula in decanatu de Lymene in parochia de Horton de eodem pro ecclesia de Brabourn

'Ex officio' case against the abbot and convent of Boxley, Kent, as a consequence of comperta in the archbishop's visitation, with respect to pasture and arable within the parish of Upchurch. Kent.

CCA DCc ChAnt/A/36/ii, p. 21

In negocio moto ex officio iuxta comperta in visitacione contra abbatem et conventum de Boxle qui percipiunt infra parochia de Oppecherch de pastura et terra arabili ad summam quingentarum acrarum. Comparuit magister Willelmus de Foderyngey procurator eorum et allegavit prescripcionem. Ad quam probandum habuit diem, et illo die nichil probavit et datum est sibi proximo [die] iuris post festum Marie Magdalene ubicumque etc. ad proponendum omnia in facto consistenc[ia] et ulterius etc. Quo die adveniente dictis abbate et conventu per fratrem Nicholaum de Wormedal confratrem et commonachum dicte domus comparentibus exhibitaque per eosdem quadam proposicione prescripcionem continente datur est prox' fidem [Fides, 6 Oct.] ad probandum eandem et ulterius etc.

Further 'ex officio' case against the abbot and convent of Boxley for failing to exhibit muniments entitling them to the appropriation of Eastchurch, Kent.

CCA DCc ChAnt/A/36/ii, p. 22

In negocio moto ex officio contra abbatem et conventum de Boxle ecclesiam de Eastchurch in proprios usus optinentes et super appropriacione illius non exhibita, comparente autem magistro Willelmo de Foderyngey procuratore eorum et uno instrumento sigillo venerabilis patris domini Walteri [Reynolds] immediati predecessoris vestre signato datus fuit dicto procuratori sextus iuris post festum sancte Marie Magdalene ad exhibendum et proponendum quicquid voluerit pro termino peremptorio, infra [this word interlined] quem diem adveniente [this word crossed out] pars exhibuit unam cartam domini Ricardi regis et pendet sub pronunciacione.

Peter, bishop of Corbavia, acts as Mepham's special commissary in a case involving suspension from church by a priest from Luddenham, Kent, and his son.

CCA DCc ChAnt/A/36/ii, p. 23 (base)

Nos Petrus permissione divina Corbaniensis episcopus et venerabilis patris domini Symonis dei gracia Cant' archiepiscopi tocius Anglie primatis commissarius in hac parte specialis Rogerum de Chilham [paroch' de Lodenham: interlined] presbiterum et Robertum filium tuum [*sic*] legitime citatos preconizatos diucius expectatos, et nullo modo comparentes, ab ingressu ecclesie suspendimus in hiis scriptis [Not concluded]

In the archbishop's presence two litigants promised to abide by the decision of arbitrators whom they were to choose jointly.

CCA DCc ChAnt/A/36/ii, p. 42
27 June [1330] Manor of Harrow

Memorandum quod quintum kalendarium Julii in claustro manerii [MS 'menerii'?] domini de Harwe presencialiter constituit coram domino Symone archiepiscopo &c. Willelmus de Pynnore et Johannes de Barnevyle consenserunt ['et promiserunt' interlined] expresse ad . . . dictum dominum quod super omni lite et discordia inter eosdem suscitatis stare ad ordinacionem nec et laudum sex personarum per eosdem eligendarum ita quod uterque predictorum tres pro parte sua eligeret . . . et nisi illi sex sic ex utraque parte electi possent in unam sentenciam concordire.

Thomas de Cobham, executor of Henry de Cobham, appoints M. John de Gloucester as his proctor.

CCA DCc ChAnt/A/36/ii, p. 42 (final entry)
26 July 1330 Croydon church

Memorandum quod vii kalendarum Augusti anno domini millesimo ccc^{mo} tricesimo in ecclesia de Croyndon [coram s . . . Brok interlined] Thomas de Cobham executor domini Henrici de Cobham constituit magistrum Johannem de Gloucestria procuratorem cum [suum? followed by illegible word] vel [illegible word] et cum potestate substituendi.

OTHER SOURCES

Summons to a provincial council in St. Paul's Cathedral.

Mandate to the bishop of London, Stephen Gravesend, as dean of the province of Canterbury.

Archbishop Simon Mepham 1328-1333: A Boy Amongst Men

Winchester Reg. Stratford, fo. 43r, edn. no 441 [Bray, *Records of Convocation* 3, pp. 101-2, prints the mandate in modern orthography from Exeter Reg. Grandisson, fo.105ᵛ]
29 November 1328 Mayfield

Symon permissione divina Cantuariensis episcopus tocius Anglie primas venerabili fratri. S. eadem gracia London' episcopo salutem et cetera. Regimini sancte Cantuariensis ecclesie dei paciencia licet inmeriti presidentes inter alias sollicitudinis nostre vigilias ad id votis ferventibus aspiramus, et mentem nostram sedulo destinamus affectu, ut ecclesia Anglicana sub pacis dulcedine vigeat, iura sua ac libertates obtinere valeat illibata gregis dominici cura vigilanti studio frequentetur cuncti quos Anglia produxit pariter et enutrit in via veritatis et iusticie dirigant gressus suos. Et presertim quod constituti in clero morum honestate refulgeant ut tanquam lucerna pedibus laicorum ipsos instruant vite merito et sermone qualiter in domo dei debeant conversari. Sane dicta ecclesia Anglicana ante hec tempora pacis turbate discrimine multis angustiis et labribus lacessita adhc modernis temporibus carbonibus odii inter proceres reaccensis maiora pericula et dispendia, nisi deus advertat, poterit verisimiliter formidare. Et super dolorem huius vulneris superadditur afflicio quo quidam filii impii et degeneres eciam et viros ecclesiasticos iniuriis innumeris afficere iura ecclesiarum et libertates malicie iaculis expugnare et quod auditui est horrendum ipsos viros ecclesiasticos mutilare trucidare aut hostiliter capere non formidant prout discurens fama denunciat et patratorum scelerum evidencia manifestat. Ad occurendum igitur tantis periculis divina clemencia suffragante et morbis premissis medicinam aliqualem prout nobis possibile fuerit adhibendum sacris canonibus eruditi et sanctissimi patris domini. J. [John] divina providencia pape XXII^di crebris monitis excitati nostrum concilium provinciale die Veneris proximo post festum Conversacionis Sancti Pauli proximo sequente in ecclesia cathedrali Sancti Pauli London' deliberato consilio ordinavimus convocandum. Quocirca vobis commitimus et mandamus quatinus omnes et singulos fratres nostros episcopos nostre Cantuariensis provincie et pro eisdem citare faciatis peremptorie decanos priores et capitula ecclesiarum cathedralium, archidiaconos abbates priores alios conventus et collegia clerumque singularum diocesium, quod iidem. episcopi decani priores ecclesiarum cathedralium archidiaconi et abbates personaliter, priores alii capitula capitula [repeated *sic*] conventus collegia singula et singulos, clerus autem cuiuslibet diocesis per duos procuratores ydoneos compareant coram nobis die et loco superius assignatis cum continuacione et prorogacione dierum sequentium usque ad finalem expedicionem agendorum nobiscum et cum fratribus nostris episcopis antedictis de premissis et aliis statum ecclesie cleri et populi correccionem excessivum morumque reformacionem contingentibus quatenus in huiusmodi provinciali concilio proferenda corrigi et reformari valeant de consuetudine vel de iure cum diligencia tractaturi et prout utilitati et honestati congruit provida deliberacione super tractandis suum consilium impensuri pariter et consensum. Proviso quod singuli episcopi antedicti antequam dioceses suas versus dictum concilium egressi fuerint cum suo clero deliberent et enquirant sagaciter de gravaminibus et defectibus dicti concilii studio reformandis quodque a clero et populo processiones fieri letanias et alias oraciones dici faciant pro pace regni et pro concilio nostro ut debitum consequatur effectum. Dictis eciam episcopis vestris litteris auctoritate nostra districtius iniungatis quatinus de die recepcionis mandati vestri in hac parte eorum singulis dirigendi, et quid fecerint in premissis et de nominibus citatorum in separatis cedulis eorum certificatoriis annectendis dictis die et loco distincte et aperte nos certificent per litteras suas patentes mandati vestri seriem continentes. Vos insuper quantum ad vos et personas vestri diocesis attinet id idem in omnibus observetis certificantes et cetera. Datum apud Maghefeld iii kalendarum Decembris anno domini millesimo CCC^{mo} vicesimo octavo et consecracionis nostre primo.

Mepham's oath excusing himself from personal involvement in the Slindon affair.

From Thorne cols. 2045 (modified orthography)
Undated [*post* 21 March 1331]

    Symon permissione divina Cantuariensis archiepiscopi tocius Anglie primas. Nunciato nobis per cancellarium nostrum quod dudum scilicet xii kal. Aprilis quidam frater Thomas de Natyndon cum quibusdam suis complicibus quorum nomina ignoramus, armis tam defensivis quam aggressivis munitis, manerium nostrum de Slyndon contra voluntatem et prohibicionem ianitoris nostri ingrederetur, et nobis existentibus in camera nostra gravi infirmitate detentis, diceret se velle modis omnibus nobis alloqui, et dicto sibi responso quod loquendi nobiscum propter infirmitatem nostrum accessus ad nos patere sibi non potuit ea vice, et propter hoc dicto monacho turbato et tam ipso quam complicibus suis ac quibusdam aliis familiaribus nostris in verbis contumeliosis prorumpentibus hinc et inde, tandem duo ex complicibus memoratis, extra portam dicti manerii vulnerati extiterant et eciam arrestati, prefatusque monachus ad sectam et uthesium quorundam quos similiter ignoramus apud Pettesworthe in libertate domini Henrici de Percy captus extitit et arestatus. Iuramus ad hec sancti Dei evangelia per nos corporaliter tacta et visa, quod hec facta vel eorum aliquod nullatenus approbamus nec rata nec ratum habemus, immo ea et eorum quodlibet penitus detestamur. Sic Deus nos adiuvet et hec sancti Dei evangelia.

Letters patent (inchoate) of Stephen Gravesend, bishop of London, testifying to the good character of Archbishop Mepham following the Slindon affair.

From Thorne cols. 2045-6 (modified orthography)
Undated [*post* 21 March 1331]

Universis presentes litteras inspecturis vel eciam audituris Stephanus permissione divina Londoniensis episcopus salutem. Odor suavissimus bona fama qua venerabilis pater dominus Simon [*spelled thus here and below*] dei gracia Cantuariensis archiepiscopus exigentibus sue probitatis meritis extollitur et laudatur Anglicanam regionem perfundit, ipsum namque dominum Simonem innocencia vite, sciencia, puritate consciencie fulgentem universaque morum honestate preclarum nimirum narrat et predicat vox communis, ut qui tanti decoris nitor eo clarius elucescat quo in communiorem deductus fuerit notionem, oraque loquentium inique a suis exinde detraccionibus conticescant.

Attestations of witnesses produced against Archbishop Mepham on behalf of the abbot by Armand de Narcès, archbishop of Aix-en-Provence, commissioned by the pope following the dishonour (infamia) inflicted on the abbot by the Slindon affair. His letter to the pope after investigation.

From Thorne col. 2046 (modified orthography)
Undated [*post* 21 March 1331]

Sanctissime pater sicut in consistorio fuerat propositum pro parte abbatis et conventus S. Augustini et eciam tanquam res notoria ad aures sanctitatis vestre devenit, quod archiepiscopus Cantuariensis tam enormiter excessit, vel officiales et familiares sui, ipso saltem audiente et forsan vidente, sciente, audiente, vel scire valente et non prohibente, licet prohibere de facili et solo verbo potuisset, non sine magno sanctitatis vestre et apostolice sedis contemptu, et in magnum preiudicium et iacturam abbatis supradicti sanctitati vestre immediate subiecti et cetera. Igitur producti fuerunt testes in attestacione abbatis xxiv et si ista causa in Anglia potuisset terminasse, de facili archiepiscopi numerum triplicasset. Et hi omnes si[n]gillatim adiurati et diligenter examinati super infamia pretacta dixerunt, quod idem archiepiscopus de ipsis excessibus in partibus illis est publice et notorie diffamatus. Et dixerunt, quod est publica vox et notorium, quod idem archiepiscopus predictos excessus fieri mandaret, et tempore quo predicti excessus commissi fuerunt sciret et audiret eos committi, et prohibere posset si vellet, et hoc de facili, et quod iuxta cameram in qua tunc erat idem archiepisopus dicti excessus fuerant commissi, et super hoc est notorie diffamatus a clericis et laicis quasi in toto regno Anglie. Dixerunt eciam, quod cum quidam frater Thomas Natindon procurator abbatis supradicti legeret scriptum citacionis in aula dictimanerii, quidam scutifer venit ad eum et dixit, 'Domine Thome quid faciatis?'. Et respondit, 'Facio que incumbunt pro iure ecclesiastico'. Et scutifer respondit, 'Et ego timeo quod morieris'. Et monachus respondit, 'Licet moriar ego prosequar iura ecclesie nostre'. Dixerunt eciam quod ipse mandavit excessus committi eosdem, pro eo quod cum alii episcopi denunciarunt de die in diem huiusmodi malefactores esse excommunicatos, ipse nunquam voluit eos vel aliquem illorum denunciare.

Itherius de Concoreto orders John de Langton, bishop of Chichester, the abbot of Waltham (Richard de Hertford) and the prior of Lewes (John de Courtenay?) and the rector of St. Julian, Sarlat diocese, to cite Archbishop Mepham following the Slindon affair.

From Thorne cols. 2047 (modified orthography)
Undated

Reverendis in Christo patribus dominis Dei gracia episcopo Cicestrie et abbati de Waltham ac religioso viro priori de Lewes Londoniensis et Cicestensis diocesis [diocesium?], rectori ecclesie sancti Juliani Carlatensis [*sic* for Sarlat . . .] Iterius de Concoreto canonicus Saresberiensis domini nostri pape et apostolice sedis in Anglia, Scocia, Wallia et Hibernia, nuncius ac iudex unicus in omnibus et singulis causis appellationum pro parte religiosorum virorum sancti Augustini subditorum parochianorumque ecclesiarum suarum sibi adherencium ad sedem apostolicam interiectarum contra reverendum patrem etc. Auctoritate apostolica qua fungimus in hac parte, vos dominum episcopum cum reverencia qua decet requirimus et monemus sub obediencia qua sedi apostolice tenemini nichilominus iniungentes, ac vobis abbati etc. et vestrum quemlibet sub poena excommunicaconis quam in vos et vestrum quemlibet canonica monicione praemissa exnunc pro tunc extunc pro nunc ferimus in hiis scriptis nisi feceritis quod mandamus, districte precipimus et mandamus, quatinus vos vel duo aut unus vestrum qui primo fuerit requisitus vel requisiti ita quod alter alterum non expectet nec alter pro altero se excuset, set qui primo fuerit requisitus huiusmodi mandatum nostrum secundum eius continenciam viriliter exequatur vel exequantur indilate. Receptis presentibus ad dictum dominum archiepiscopum si ad eum vobis tutus videatur accessus, accedatis, sin autem publice in eius ecclesia Cantuarie vel curia auctoritate nostra citetis legitime quod compareat etc. Intimantes eidem, quod sive veniret sive non, in dictis causis et negociis procedemus prout iuris fuerit, eius absencia vel contumacia non obstante.

Letters patent of Itherius de Concoreto 'sedens pro tribunali' incorporating his sentence against the contumacious archbishop.

From Thorne cols. 2048-9 (modified orthography). This should be compared with the the judgment given in *Lit. Cant.* i. no. 483, which is dated 13 November 1332. [Undated]

In Dei nomine Amen. Universis presentes literas etc. Itherius de Concoreto etc. Dudum sanctissimus pater dominus Johannes divina providencia papa XXII etc. Significarunt nobis dilecti filii abbas et conventus sancti Augustini Cantuarie et infra. Nos eundem dominum Simonem Cantuariensem archiepiscopum reputamus iusticia exigente contumacem, et in eius contumacia Dei et domini nostri Jhesu Christi nomine invocato eiusque sacrosanctis evangeliis positis coram nobis, ut de vultu Deo nostrum prodeat iudicium et oculi nostri videat equitatem, et ut dicti archiepiscopi contumacia Dei presencia inpleatur, habito super hoc consilio peritorum, nobiscum eciam plena deliberacione omnibus discussis, propositis, productis et probatis, diffinitivam sentenciam in causis et negociis huiusmodi in hiis scriptis proferimus, et in modum qui sequitur et formam. In primis quoniam constat nobis per inspeccionem privilegiorum felicis recordacionis Romanorum pontificum, et specialiter Bonifacii pape viii eisdem religiosis et eorum monasterio concessorum evidenter, dictos religiosos cum omnibus membris suis, iuribus et pertinenciis et personis ubicumque constitutis fore liberos et exemptos ab omni dominio et potestate archiepiscopi Cantuariensis et quorumcumque iudicum ordinariorum et soli Romano pontifici subiectos ita quod nec idem archiepiscopus iure metropolitico seu diocesano aut legationis vel tuicionis pretextu quas in Cantuariensi provincia habere se asserit, in predictum monasterium aut membra aut bona ad ipsos spectancia et que in posterum spectarent, et in personas eis subiectas utpote libera et exempta et prefate sancte sedi immediate subiecta posset

Archbishop Simon Mepham 1328-1333: A Boy Amongst Men

nullatenus iurisdiccionem aliqualem exercere, et quod per deposiciones testium in causa huiusmodi productorum probatum extitit evidenter, et dicti religiosi et predecessores sui in possessione exempcionis sunt et fuerunt pacifice et quiete, scientibus et patientibus archiepiscopis Cantuariensibus per tempus et per tempora. Probatumque est eciam, quod venerabilis pater dominus Simon Cantuariensis archepiscopi plenam habet noticiam exempcionis et privilegiorum loco et tempore competenti, unde deliberacione diligenti nobiscum habita, dictos religiosos et eorum monasterium, cum omnibus ecclesiis et membris suis et personis sibi subiectis, in iure et possessione libertatis et exempcionis huiusmodi, in hiis scriptis auctoritate apostolica nobis in hac parte commissa sentencialiter et diffinitive pronunciamus tanquam sufficienter munitos, fore tuendos et defendendos, et ab inquietacione dicti archiepiscopi super premissis ipsos absolvimus, et eosdem bene et legitime provocasse, archiepiscopum vero male et inique processisse, dictoque archiepiscopo super premissis perpetuum silentium imponentes. Omnes vero processus erga dictos religiosos et eorum subditos factos et habitos per dictum archiepiscopum, officiales seu commissarios suos pronunciamus et declaramus sentencialiter et diffinitive fore iniuriosos et iniustos, suasque citaciones vagas et incertas, ipsosque processus et excommunicacionis sentencias si que occasione ipsorum late fuerunt nullos et irritos, et quatenus de facto processerunt cassamus, annullamus et irritamus, dictosque religiosos pronunciamus et declaramus sentencialiter et diffinitive a dictis iniuriosis processibus bene et legitime appellasse, et dictum archiepiscopum et suos perperam et inique processisse, dictumque archiepiscopum in expensis legitimis eisdem religiosis per hanc nostram sentenciam diffinitivam condempnamus earum taxacione nobis inposterum reservata.

Appendix 6

THE CONTEMPORARY EPISCOPATE

CANTERBURY PROVINCE

ENGLISH SEES

Bath & Wells

John Droxford (Drokensford), 1309-29 (ob. 9 May)

Ralph of Shrewsbury, D.Th., D.Cn.L., 1329-1363

Chichester

John Langton, 1305-37

Coventry & Lichfield

Roger Northburgh, M., 1321-58 (cons. 1322)

Ely

John Hothum, 1316-37

Archbishop Simon Mepham 1328-1333: A Boy Amongst Men

Exeter

John Grandisson, 1327-1369

Hereford

Thomas Charlton, Lic.Th., 1327-44

Lincoln

Henry Burghersh, 1320-40

London

Stephen Gravesend, M., 1319-38

Norwich

William Ayrminne (Airmyn), 1325-36

Rochester

Hamo de Hethe, 1319-52

Salisbury

Roger Martival, D.Th., 1315-30 (d. 14 Mar.)
Robert Wyville, 1330-75

Winchester

John Stratford, D.C.L.,1323-33

Worcester

Adam Orleton, D.Cn.L., 1327-33

WELSH SEES

Bangor
Matthew de Englefield, M., (Madoc ap Iowerth), 1328-37

Llandaff
John de E(a)glescliff, OP., 1323-1347

St. Asaph's
Dafydd ap Bleddyn, M., 1315-46

St. David's
Henry de Gower, D.Cn. & C.L., 1328-1347

YORK PROVINCE

York
William Melton, 1317-40

Carlisle
John Ross, DCL, 1325-32
John de Kirkby, O.Can.S.A., 1332-52

Durham
Louis de Beaumont, 1317-33

Bibliography

MANUSCRIPT SOURCES

CAMBRIDGE

Corpus Christi College (CCC)
MS. 174 English version of Brut chronicle

Trinity College (TCC)
R.5 41 Canterbury based chronicle, continuation of Gervase

CANTERBURY CATHEDRAL ARCHIVES

Dean and Chapter of Canterbury (DCc)

Chartae antiquae:

A/36/i Act Book. Fragments from Audience Court business temp. Abp Reynolds, Cathedral Priory acting *sede vacante*, and Abp. Mepham (July 1328-June 1329)
A/36/ii Act Book (*Registrum Actorum*). Mepham's Audience Court (1328-30)
C/231-1328. Prior Henry Eastry and the chapter of Canterbury Cathedral priory to Pope John XXII, informing him of the appointment of Brothers Geoffrey

Poterel and John Everard as proctors for confirmation of Mepham's election as archbishop.

S/392 5 April 1328. Prior Eastry announces the election of Mepham *via compromissi*
Registers: G, I, L, Q

CHIPPENHAM

Wiltshire and Swindon History Centre
D1/2/3-4. Bishop Robert Wyville's register.

DURHAM

Durham University Library
D. A. Harding, M.Litt thesis (1985), 'The regime of Isabella and Mortimer 1326-30'

LINCOLN

Lincolnshire Archives Office
Reg. Henry Burghersh (1320-40) 1-3 (Regs. 4-5, 5b)

LONDON

British Library (BL)
Harleian MS 1729, fo. 133r. Discord between Mepham and his suffragans (Hearne's Hemingford)
Add. MSS.
6066 Andrew Coltée Ducarel, *Fragmenta sequentia registrorum Simonis de Mepeham et Johannis de Stratford Cantuar' archiepiscoporum* (1756)
6159 Lengths of archiepiscopates

Cotton MSS:

Claudius A.v, Peterborough chronicle
Faustina B.v., Historia Roffensis (HR)
Lambeth Palace Library

MSS.

20, fo. 182r Martyrology of Christ Church. Mepham's legacy by hand of M. Laurence Fastolf (Cf. BL Arundel MS. 68)
99 *Vitae Arch. Cant.* ('Birchington' and other material); 1106

The National Archives (TNA, formerly PRO)

Chancery:

C53 Charter Rolls
C143/195/8 Inquisitions ad Quod Damnum
Edmund de Mepham, Simon de Mepham, and John de la Dene to grant a messuage, mills, land, and rent in East Malling, Birling, Northfleet, Meopham, and Hoo to a chaplain in the chapel of St. James of la Dene in Meopham, retaining lands in Meopham and Luddesdown. 1327/1328.

King's Bench:

KB27/275 m.12 (re Maidstone rectory)
KB27/276/Rex (re John Stratford)

Special Collections:

SC7/56/19 Papal Bulls (*CPL* 2, 1305-42, p. 272). Request to Edward [III.] to take into his favour Simon [de Mepham], rector of Tunstall [Kent], whose election as archbishop of Canterbury by the prior and chapter of that church, the pope has confirmed. *Divine retributionis premium* ... Avignon. 6 Id. (8th) Jun., 1328.

Access to Archives (A2A). Document ref. no. p339/28/1. Centre for Kentish Studies, *Inspeximus* and confirmation to Abp. Edmund Grindal by Elizabeth I, 1575-6, of Edward III's charter, Waltham, 6 February 1331-2, to Simon de Mepham, Archbishop of Canterbury granting a market on Mondays and a fair for five days at Michaelmas at his manor of Smarden.

SC8/97/4840. Petition to king about encroachments by the Barons of the Cinq Ports in Kent

SC8/197/9806. Letter to king re purgation of a priest indicted for stealing horses requesting that his goods be returned to him

SC8/236/11780. Mepham requests the king that Edmund de Neville may be removed from occupation of the church of Great Horkesley, Essex

Transcript:

31/9/17A Extracts from Andreas Sapiti's register, fos. 80r-85r, 100r-103v

NORWICH

Norfolk Record Office
'Confirmation and settlements of peculiar jurisdiction', nos. 2757, 3854-5

ROME, ITALY

Vatican Archives

RA Registra Avenionensia:

30, fos. 443v-44r. Loan re Mepham's curial obligation of £2,000, 23 June 1328
31, fo. 122v. Mepham's petition requesting exemption from sentences fulminated against him for non-appearance elsewhere while resident in his manors, 14 July 1328 fo. 130v, permission to interrupt visitation while on papal or royal business, and to resume it thereafter. 14 July 1328
32, fo. 27v. Pope re John 'le Orfreyeser' claiming to be abbot of Faversham. 30 Aug. 1328. [He is supposed to have resigned in 1325 as guilty of dilapidation and simony. *Heads of Religious Houses*, p. 45.]
36, fo. 538v. Mepham pays what he owes for common services (*pro complememto sui communis servicii cameram contingentis*) by hand of Alexander de Bardis of the Bardi of Florence. 6 Nov. 1329

WARWICK

Warwickshire Record Office CR 136/C2027. Archbishop Melton's letter.

WINCHESTER

Hampshire Record Office
Reg. John Stratford, 21M65/A1/5 [Win.R.S.]

PRINTED SOURCES

Chronicles
Adae Murimuth, Continuatio Chronicarum, ed. E. Maunde Thompson (Rolls Ser., 1889)
Anglia Sacra see *Willielmi de Dene Historia Roffensis*

Annales Paulini, in *Chronicles of the Reigns of Edward I and Edward II,* ed. W. Stubbs, 2 vols. (Rolls Ser. 1882-3)

Chronica Guillelmi Thorne in *Historiae Anglicanae Scriptores Decem,* ed. Roger Twysden (London, 1652)

Chronicon Galfridi le Baker de Swynebroke, ed. E. Maunde Thompson, (Oxford 1889)

Chronicon Henrici Knighton, ed. J.R. Lumby (Rolls Ser., 1889, 1895)

Concilia Magnae Britanniae et Hiberniae, ed. D. Wilkins, 4 vols. (London, 1737)

Willielmi de Dene Historia Roffensis, ed. H. Wharton [with significant omissions], in *Anglia Sacra* i. pp. 356-77 (London 1691) [BL Cotton MS Faustina B.V]

Collections of Documents, Registers, and Calendars

A Biographical Register of the University of Oxford to 1500, 3 vols. (Oxford, 1957-9),

Emden, A. B. [*Biog. Oxon.*]

Calendar of the Plea and Memoranda Rolls . . . of the City of London 1323-1364, ed. A.H. Thomas (Cambridge, 1926)

Councils and Synods II, ed. F.M. Powicke and C.R. Cheney, 2 vols. (Oxford, 1964)

Documents Illustrative of English History in the Thirteenth and Fourteenth Centuries, London 1844

Heads of Religious Houses, see Secondary Sources s.v. Smith

John Le Neve, *Fasti Ecclesiae Anglicanae* 12 vols. (London, 1962-67)

A List of Monumental Brasses in the British Isles (London, 1964), comp. Mill Stephenson

List of Monumental Brasses remaining in the County of Kent in 1922, with notes of some lost examples (London, n.d.), R. Griffin, Mill Stephenson

Literae Cantuarienses, ed. J. B. Sheppard, 3 vols. (Rolls Ser. 1887-1889).

Monasticon Anglicanum, ed. W. Dugdale rev. J. Caley et al., 6 vols. in 8 (London, 1817-30)

Munimenta Academica [*Oxon.*] 2 vols. (Rolls Ser 1868)

Records of Convocation III, Canterbury 1313-1377, ed. G. Bray (Woodbridge 2005)

The Register of John de Grandisson, Bishop of Exeter (A.D. 1327-1369), 3 vols. [consecutive pagination], ed. F.C. Hingeston-Randolph (London/Exeter, 1894, 1897, 1899)

The Register of John de Stratford, Bishop of Winchester, 1323-1333, 2 vols., ed R. M Haines, Surrey Record Society (Bristol 2010-11)

The Register of Richard de Swinfield, ed. W.W. Capes (Hereford, 1909)

Registrum Hamonis Hethe, 2 vols., ed. Charles Johnson (Oxford, 1948)

Registrum Radulphi Baldock, Gilberti Segrave, Ricardi Newport, et Stephani Gravesend, ed. R. C. Fowler (London, 1911)

Registrum Roffense, ed. J. Thorpe (London, 1769)

Series Episcoporum Ecclesiae Catholicae Occidentalis, Ser. VI Britannia etc. Tomus 1 Ecclesia Scoticana, ed. D.E.R. Watt (Stuttgart, 1991)

Secondary Sources

Barlow, F., 'A View of Archbishop Lanfranc', *JEH* 16 (1965), pp 163-77

—*The English Church 1066-1154*, (London/New York 1979)

Boyle, L. E., 'William of Pagula and the *Speculum Regis* Edwardi III', *Mediaeval Studies* 32 (1970), pp. 329-36

Bray, G. ed., *Records of Convocation III, Canterbury 1313-1377*, Woodbridge 2005

Bryant, R., Heighway, C., Bryant, R., *The Tomb of Edward II: a royal monument in Gloucester Cathedral*, Past Historic n.d.

Cam, H.M., 'The General Eyres of 1329-30' in *Liberties and Communities in Medieval England*, pp. 150-62 (reprinted from *EHR* 39 (1924), pp. 241-52).

Canon Law of the Church of England, Being the Report of the Archbishops' Commission ..., London 1947

Cheney, C.R., *English Synodalia of the Thirteenth Century* (Oxford, 1941)

—*Medieval Texts and Studies*, (Oxford 1973). [This includes 'Textual Problems of the English Provincial Canons', pp. 111-37; 'William Lyndwood's *Provinciale*'.

pp. 158-84; 'Some Aspects of Diocesan Legislation during the Thirteenth Century', pp. 185-202.]

Cheney, M., *Roger, Bishop of Worcester, 1164-1179,* Oxford 1980

Churchill, I. J., *Canterbury Administration,* 2 vols. London 1933

Cuttino, G.T., Lyman, G.W., "Where is Edward II", *Speculum* 53 (1978), pp. 522-44.

Duggan, C., *Twelfth Century Decretal Collections,* London, 1963

Edwards, K., 'Bishops and Learning during the reign of Edward II', *Church Quarterly Review* cxxxviii (1944), pp. 57-86

Gibbs, M., Lang, J., *Bishops and Reform 1215-1272,* Oxford 1934

Golding-Bird, C. H., *The History of Meopham,* London 1914

Haines, R.M., *Archbishop John Stratford,* Pontifical Institute of Mediaeval Studies, Toronto 1986 (*Abp. Stratford*)

—'An Innocent Abroad: The Career of Simon Mepham, Archbishop of Canterbury 1328-1333', *EHR* 112 (1997), pp. 555-96

—'Bishops and Politics in the Reign of Edward II: Hamo de Hethe, Henry Wharton, and the *Historia Roffensis*', *JEH* 44 (1993), pp. 586-609

—'Conflict in Government: Archbishops versus Kings', in *Aspects of Late Medieval Government and Society,* ed. J.G. Rowe, Toronto 1986, pp. 213-45

—*Ecclesia anglicana: Studies in the English Church of the Later Middle Ages,* Toronto 1989 [*EA*]

—'*Edwardus Redivivus,* the "Afterlife" of Edward of Caernarvon', *TB&GAS* 114 (1996), pp. 65-86

—'Some criticisms of Bishops in the Fourteenth and Fifteenth Centuries', in *Miscellanea Historiae Ecclesiasticae* 8, ed. B. Vogler, *BRHE* 72, Louvain, Bruxelles 1987, pp. 169-80

—'Some Sermons at Hereford Attributed to Archbishop John Stratford', *JEH* 34 (1989), pp. 425-37.

—'Sumptuous Apparel for a Royal Prisoner: Archbishop Melton's Letter, 14 January 1330', *EHR* 124 (2009), pp. 885-94

—'The Administration of the Diocese of Worcester *Sede Vacante*, 1266-1350', *JEH* 13 (1962), pp. 156-71

—'The Episcopate during the reign of Edward II and the Regency of Mortimer and Isabella', *JEH* 56 (2005), pp. 657-709

—'The Episcopate of a Benedictine monk: Hamo de Hethe bishop of Rochester (1317-1352)', *Revue Bénédictine* 102 (1992), pp. 102-207

—*The Register of John de Stratford Bishop of Winchester, 1323-1333*, 2 vols. Surrey Record Society 2010, 2011]

—'The Release of Ornaments in the Archbishop's chapel and some other arrangements following Simon Mepham's elevation', *Archaeologia Cantiana* 122 (2002), pp. 363-71

—'The Stamford Council of April 1327', *EHR* 112 (2007), pp. 141-5

Helmholz, R. H., *The Oxford History of the Laws of England: Volume 1 The Canon Law and Ecclesiastical Jurisdictiom from 597 to the 1640s*, Oxford 2004

Holmes, G.A., 'The Rebellion of the Earl of Lancaster, 1328-9', *Bulletin of the Institute of Historical Research* xxviii (1955), 84-9

Hussey, A., *Some Account of the Parish Church of Wingham*, 1891

Ker, Neil, *Medieval Libraries of Great Britain*, London 1964

Konrath, M., The Poems of William of Shoreham, *EETS* 86 (1902), from BL Add. MS 17376.

Levison, W., *England and the Continent in the Eighth Century*, Oxford 1946

Lobel, M.D., 'A detailed account of the 1327 rising at Bury St. Edmund's and the subsequent trial', *Suffolk Institute of Archaeology and Natural History* 21 (1933), pp. 215-31

Lunt, W. E., *Financial Relations of The Papacy with England 1327-1534*, Mediaeval Academy of America, Cambridge Mass. 1962

Marchant, G., *Edward II in Gloucestershire 'A King in our Midst'*, 2007

McHardy, A.K., 'The Loss of Archbishop Stratford's register', *Historical Research* 70 (1997), pp. 337-41

Miller, E., *The Abbey and Bishopric of Ely*, Cambridge 1951 repr. 1969

Morey, A., *Bartholomew of Exeter,* Cambridge 1937.

Mortimer, I., *The Greatest Traitor, the Life of Sir Roger Mortimer,* Pimlico, London 2004

—*The Perfect King, the Life of Edward III,* London 2008

Ormrod, W.M., 'Agenda for Legislation, 1322-c.1340', *EHR* 105 (1990), pp. 1-33.

—*The Reign of Edward III,* New Haven/London 1990

Parkin, C.A., 'Wingham, a Medieval Town', *Arch. Cant.* 93 (1977), pp. 61-79

Parry, C.H., *The Parliaments and Councils of England,* London 1839

Pascoe, L.B., *Jean Gerson: Principles of Church Reform,* Leiden 1973

Sayers, J. E., *Papal Judges Delegate in the Province of Canterbury 1198-1254,* Oxford 1971

Smith, D.M., London V.C.M., *The Heads of Religious Houses: England and Wales II. 1216-1377,* Cambridge 2001

Thompson, A.H., *The English Clergy,* Oxford 1947

Ullmann, W., *Principles of Government and Politics in the Middle Ages,* 2nd edn. London 1966

—*The Growth of Papal Government in the Middle Ages,* 2nd edn. London 1962 repr. 1965

Verduyn, Anthony, 'The Politics of Law and Order during the Early Years of Edward III', *EHR* 108 (1993), pp. 842-67

Wheeler, H., 'William de Shoreham', *Arch. Cant.* 108 (1990), pp. 153-61, and see Konrath above

Wright, J. R., *The Church and the English Crown 1305-1334,* Toronto 1980

—'The Supposed Illiteracy of Archbishop Walter Reynolds', *Studies in Church History* 5 (1969), pp. 58-68

General Index

Note: Bishops' dates from consecration

A

Abingdon abbey 12, 61
Agnes, lady of Askerswell *see* Askerswell, church of
Aldon, Thomas de 35
alien religious 12
Aller, church of 101
Amport, Hampshire 91 *see also* Winchester: diocese of
Antwerp 14, 16, 87, 119-20
archbishops versus kings 22 n. 1
Askerswell, church of 101
Astley, Thomas de, archdeacon of Middlesex 98
audience court records 87-101
auditors of causes:
   Badesley *see* Badesley, John de
   Canterbury *see* Canterbury, Thomas de
   Haut *see* Haut, Richard de
   Weston *see* Weston, Robert de: as auditor of causes
Audley, Hugh de, earl of Gloucester 34, 37
Augustinian canon 5
Aumberleye, John de 75, 99
Avignon 25 n. 31, 50, 55 n. 7, 71, 77 n. 23, 83, 90, 126
   Dominican church at 15

Mepham's consecration at 15, 87
Aymericus *see* Rogesio, Aymericus (Aymer) de, rector of St. Julian
Ayrminne (Ayermine; Airmyn), bishop of Norwich (1325–36) 5, 61, 70, 93

B

Badesley, John de 124
Badlesmere, Lady 38
Bannockburn, Battle of 37
Bardi, the 15, 21
Barlings near Lincoln 14
Barnet, John, bishop of Ely (1366–73) 22 n. 2
Barnevyle, John de 92, 132
Barnstaple, archdeacon of 60
Barown, Godfrey (Geoffrey) 74
Bateman, William, bishop of Norwich (1344–55) 54
Bath and Wells diocese 73
   bishops of:
     Droxford *see* Droxford (Drokensford), John, bishop of Bath and Wells (1309–29)
     Shrewsbury *see* Shrewsbury, Ralph of, bishop of Bath and Wells (1329–63)
     visitation of 50-1, 53 *see also* Wells Cathedral: visitation of

Beaconsfield, church of 95
Beaumes (Bishop Orleton's manor) 95
Beaumont, Henry de 34
Beaumont, Louis de, bishop of Durham (1317–33) 4
Beauvais 71
Beddington, church of 96
Bedford 34-6, 43 n. 27
Bek, Antony, bishop of Durham (1284–1311) 17
Bek, Thomas, lawyer-bishop of Ely (1341–7) 22, 22 n. 2
Bemenstre, John de 101
Benedictine vows 20
Bereford, Simon de 35
Berkeley castle 29
Bermondsey Priory, prior of 73
Bertinus, St, feast of 16
Birling, Kent 10
Birston, William de, archdeacon of Gloucester 17
Bishopsbourne, church of 124
Bleddyn, Dafydd ap, bishop of St. Asaph (1315–46) 4, 142
Bloyou (Bloyon), John de 38, 44 n. 37
Bodeston, William de 101
Boniface of Savoy, archbishop of Canterbury (1245–70) 2, 54, 90
Boniface VIII, pope (1295–1303) 44 n. 40, 64, 76 n. 5
Bosco, Stephen de 38
Botherton, Thomas of, earl of Norfolk 29, 32-5
Boxley Abbey 130-1
Boyle, Leonard E. 36
Brabant 14, 16, 87
Brabourne, Kent 130
Bradwardine, Thomas de, archbishop of Canterbury (1349) 9, 79
Brampton, Richard de, rector of Earls Barton 89
Brasted, church of 10, 12
    indent of Edmund de Mepham's brass in 10, 10 i., 22 n. 7
Bremelham, William de 100
Bridge, rural dean of 73
Bristol, chapel of St. Giles's relationship with 89 see also St. Giles chapel
Brok (Brook), Robert 18, 38, 48
Brutony, William, rector of Honiton (Honiton Courtney) 100
bulls, papal 15, 50, 64, 73, 76, 83, 87, 90, 92, 95, 126
Burghersh, Henry, bishop of Lincoln (1320–40) 4-5, 12, 14-15, 25 n. 32, 31, 43 n. 27, 70, 89, 91, 94
Burghton, Hugh de 40, 92
Bury St. Edmund's Abbey 61-2

C

Caernarvon (Caernarfon), Edward of see Edward II, king of England
Canterbury:
    archbishop's palace in 16
    churches in:
        St. Alphege's 125, 127
        St. Paul's 63
    Court of 61, 82, 86
    deanery of 39, 73
    official of the archdeacon of 73
    province of 1-2, 9, 18, 48, 50, 70, 89, 91, 140
    dean of (bishop of London) 30, 33, 37, 55, 70, 132, 135
    visitation of 38-9, 46-8
Canterbury, Richard de, monk of St. Augustine's 66, 74
Canterbury, Thomas de 18, 38, 97, 123-4
    acts in audience court 97
Canynggs, William de 75
Carlisle, see of 1, 4-5, 70
Ceccano, Annibaldo Gaetani da, cardinal 20
chancellor:
    archiepiscopal see Hockley (Hockele), Thomas de

of Oxford University *see* Harclay, Henry de
royal
  Burghersh *see* Burghersh, Henry, bishop of Lincoln (1320-40)
  Hothum *see* Hothum, John, bishop of Ely (1316-37)
  Stratford *see* Stratford, John: as royal chancellor
Chardstock, Devon 50
Charing
  archbishop's manor of 89, 125
  church of 125
  rural dean of 73
Charing, Simon de 16, 38-9
Charlton, Thomas, bishop of Hereford (1327–44) 5, 141
Charlton Mackrell, Somerset 92
Charlwood, Surrey *see* Cornhull, William de
Chart, Kent 23, 82, 99-100
  vicar of *see* Shoreham (Shorham), William de
Chartham, Kent:
  archiepiscopal manor of 16, 119
  church of 125
Chatham, Kent 87
Chaumbre, John de la 120
Chelesham, William de 49
Cheney, C. R. 4, 7 n. 12, 109 n. 1
Chester 14
Chesterford, Essex 89
Chichester 10, 87
  bishop of *see* Langton, John, bishop of Chichester (1305–37)
  diocese of 67-8, 70, 89
  visitation of 50, 53
Chichester Cathedral 12-13
Chilham, Roger de 131
Chillenden, Adam de, prior of Canterbury 15
Chislet, church of 64
Christ Church, Canterbury 71, 74-5, 97, 122, 125
  apostolic privileges of 19, 63-4
  appointment of obedientiaries 38, 99

books given by Mepham to 23
chapels in 75
chapter house election in 13-15
Mepham's visitation of *see* Canterbury: visitation of
ordinations in *see* ordinations
priors of:
  Eastry *see* Eastry, Henry de, prior of Canterbury
  Oxenden *see* Oxenden, Richard de, prior of Canterbury
  sacrist of *see* Sancta Margareta, Hugh de, sacrist of Christ Church
Chudleigh, Devon 60
Churchill, I. J. 54, 87
Cinq Ports 40, 100
Cirencester, John of 19
Clare, Gilbert de, earl de Gloucester (ob. 1314) 37, 44 n. 34
Claxton, William de, prior of Norwich (1326–44) 54, 93
Cliffe-by-Higham, Kent 90
Clinton, William de, earl of Huntingdon 37
Clyvedon, John de 101
Cobham, Sir Henry de 37, 40, 132
Cobham, Thomas de
  bishop of Worcester (1317–27) 8, 15
  executor of Henry de Cobham 132
Coleshull, John de, rector of Nuneham Courtenay 12
Colwell, Thomas, monk of St. Augustine's 66
Concoreto, Itherius (Itier) de, canon of Salisbury 64, 67, 73, 84, 93-4, 98-9, 137-8
constitutions:
  Digest, the 59, 98
  diocesan 2
  papal Debent 44 n. 40
  provincial 2, 4, 6, 61, 98
Corbaria, Peter (Petro) de 90
Corbavia (Corbaviensis), Peter de (or of Bologna) 18-19, 88, 90, 122, 131
Cornhull, William de 101

Cornubia, John de 71
Cornubia, Philip de, archdeacon of Salop 23 n. 14
Cornwall:
  archdeacon of 60
  record office of 57 n. 23, 94
Cotley in Chardstock parish (manor of Isabel de Cotteley) 50
Coule, John de, rector of Great Horkesley 40, 90
councils:
  provincial 38, 59, 98, 132
  St. Paul's 32, 88
  royal:
    London 1
    Nottingham 1
Courtenay (Curtenay), John de, prior of Lewes, of Tavistock 72, 77 n. 16, 137
Coventre, William de, monk de Canterbury 71
Craneford, William de 99
Crantock (Krantock), college of 60
Crewkerne, church of 101 *see also* Bodeston, William de
Crokford, John de, rector of Wittersham 16
Croscombe, Devon 96
Crowthorne, William de 95
Croydon, Surrey 90
  bailiwick of 120
  church of 125, 132
  exempt deanery of 98
Curia, Papal or Roman 14-18, 25 n. 44, 50, 54, 55 n. 7, 66, 70-1, 74-5, 77 n. 23, 120, 125
Curtlington, William de, abbot of Westminster 19

D

Darnford, Suffolk 88
Dartford, rural dean of 49, 65
Deal, Kent 93
Dene, the reputed vii

Dene, Joan de la *see* Mepham, Joan
Dene, John de la 10
Dene, William, archdeacon of Rochester 17, 31, 35, 37, 46, 55 n. 4, 61
Dogmersfield, church of 97
Dover, Kent 14, 16, 37, 87, 119 *see also* St. Radegund's (Bradsole) Abbey
Dover, Robert de, monk of Canterbury 13
Downton (manor of the bishops of Winchester) 31
Droxford (Drokensford), John, bishop of Bath and Wells (1309–29) 4, 140
Durant, Peter de 75
Durham:
  see of 1-2, 4, 6 n. 4, 17
  visitation of priory of 44 n. 40
Dyneham, John de 95

E

E(a)glescliff (Eclescliff), John de, bishop of Llandaff (1323–47) 5, 142
Earls Barton, Northampton 89 *see also* Brampton, Richard de, rector of Earls Barton
East Lavant, Sussex 89
East Malling, Kent 10
East Wickham, chapel of 65
Eastbridge hospital 26
Eastchurch, Kent 131
Eastry, church of 39, 45 n. 41
Eastry, Henry de, prior of Canterbury 13, 16, 18-20, 30, 33, 37, 39, 54, 59-60, 82, 88, 96
ecclesiastical ornaments 16, 43, 87-8, 120-1
Edington, Wiltshire 94
Edmund 22 n. 6, 25 n. 44
Edward I, king of England 11-12
Edward II, king of England 3, 6 n. 10, 13, 15, 41 n. 2, 41 n. 5, 41
  alleged survival of 81, 85 n. 3

death of 28-9
tomb of 29, 41 n. 5, 41 n. 6
Edward III, king of England 5, 13-15, 28-9, 41 n. 4, 44 n. 33, 77 n. 23, 82, 92, 94
Elmham, John de 34
Eltham, Kent 20, 91, 115
Ely:
   Benedictine monastery at 1
   bishopric of 1, 4, 70
Englefield, Matthew de (Madoc ap Iowerth), bishop of Bangor (1328–37) 142
episcopate, background and education of the 1-2
Erith, court held in church of 65
Esher, Surrey 91
Essche, Thomas de 92
Essex 34
   sheriff of 40, 90
Estune, Thomas de 75
Everard, John, monk and proctor of Canterbury 14
Exeter:
   archdeacon of 60
   bishop of *see* Grandisson, John, bishop of Exeter (1327–69)
   cathedral chapter of 60, 97
   depredation in diocese of 28, 41 n. 3
   visitation of 39, 50, 84, 97
Eye, Simon of, abbot of Ramsey 36

F

Farnham, Ralph de 100
Fastolf, Laurence, canon of St. Paul's 38, 44 n. 38, 48, 90, 99, 124, 127
   as Mepham's executor 38, 75, 77 n. 23, 84
   as Mepham's treasurer 18
Faversham, church of 63, 76 n. 2
Faversham, Symon de, will of 129
Faversham Abbey:
   abbot of 37
   subcollector of tenth 92
Fissheburn, William de 14

Fitzpayne (Ftzpain), Ela 51-3, 96-7
Flemyng, John 129
Florence, Bardi of *see* Bardi, the
Foderyngey, William de 130-1
Forde, John de 52
Frampton, Dorset 94
Frekenham (Freckenham, Suffolk?) 49
Frendesbury, John de, rector of Bromley 47
Frome Billet, Dorset 101 *see also* Bemenstre, John de
Fyndon, William de 75
Fysshebourne, William de 129

G

Galenon, John 101
Galloway (Whithorn; Candida Casa), bishopric of 1
Gaveston, Piers 23
Ghent (Gandavo), Simon of, bishop of Salisbury (1297–1315) 17
Glastonbury Abbey 95
   abbot of *see* Sodbury, Adam of, abbot of Glastonbury (1323–34)
Gloucester 33
   archdeacon of *see* Birston, William de, archdeacon of Gloucester
   earls of 16, 37 *see also* Clare, Gilbert de, earl de Gloucester (ob. 1314)
Gloucester, John de 132
Golding-Bird, C. H. 11, 23 n. 10, 44 n. 38, 150
Goring, Sussex 99
Gower, Henry de, bishop of St. David's (1328–47) 5, 142
Grandisson, John, bishop of Exeter (1327–69) 4, 18, 28, 38, 50, 60-1, 62 n. 7, 73, 82, 86 n. 11, 133
Gravesend, Kent 9, 16, 87
Gravesend, Stephen, bishop of London (1319–38) 4, 32, 34, 37, 40, 55 n. 4, 60, 70, 81, 91, 95, 119, 132, 135
Great Horkesley 40, 90

Greneweye, Thomas de, monk of Canterbury 13
Grosseteste, Robert, bishop of Lincoln (1235–53) 2
Grove, John de 66

H

Hakendon, Stephen de, monk of St. Augustine's 72
Halling (bishop of Rochester's manor) 28, 49, 56, 61
Hampshire, sheriff of *see* Southampton, sheriff of
Hanonia (Hanover) 120
Harclay, Henry de 12, 16, 23 n. 16
Harrow (archbishop's manor) 92, 125, 132
Hasstheland, Hugh de 128
Hatfield by Charing, manor of 38
Haut, Richard de 124
Hawkchurch, Dorset 100
Hayes, Kent or Middlesex 91
Henry, rector of Patching 88
Henry, earl of Lancaster 29-31, 33-4, 36, 41 n. 4, 42 n. 14, 43 n. 27, 79
Henry I, king of England 1
Henry III, king of England 2
Henxeye, Henry de, monk of Rochester 57
Hertford, Richard de, abbot of Waltham (1308–45) 72, 137
Hervey, bishop of Bangor (1092–1109), of Ely (1109–31) 1
Hethe (Hythe), Hamo de, bishop of Rochester (1319–52) 4-5, 20, 28, 32, 37, 44, 46-50, 55 n. 2, 55 n. 8, 13, 56 n. 15, 61, 75, 79-81, 90-1, 95-7
Higham Ferrers (Lancastrian manor) 30, 42 n. 10
Hinton, Dorset 52, 97
Historia Roffensis (Dene, reputed) 12, 41 n. 2, 46-7, 55 n. 2, 55
Hockley (Hockele), Thomas de 17-18, 44 n. 37, 126

Holy Cross, college of 60
Holy Trinity, church of 100
Honiton (Honiton Courtney), Dorset 100 *see also* Brutony, William, rector of Honiton (Honiton Courtney)
Hoo, Kent 11
Horton-by-Windsor, church of 89, 125
Horton Priory, prior of 73, 130
Hothum, John, bishop of Ely (1316–37) 4-5, 70
Hova Villa, prebend of *see* Chichester Cathedral
Hunstane, Godefrey 120

I

Ickham, Richard de, monk of Canterbury 13
Isabella, queen of Edward II 5-6, 13-15, 34-5
    letter on behalf of Mepham 24 n. 27
    regime with Mortimer 28-31, 33-4, 41 n. 1, 80
Isle of Wight 12
Islep (Islip), Simon, archbishop of Canterbury (1349–66) 36, 43 n. 31, 58 n. 35, 93
Ivingho, Nicholas de, monk of Canterbury 14

J

John, prior of the Augustinian house of St. Gregory 76
John XXII, pope (1316–34) 8, 14, 20, 50, 59, 64, 90, 126

K

Kennington, church of 64
Kent 9-12, 16, 22 n. 7
    archbishop's manors in 21, 28, 38, 75, 82
    earl of *see* Woodstock, Edmund of, earl of Kent
    royal justices in:
        Cobham *see* Cobham, Sir Henry de

Archbishop Simon Mepham 1328-1333: A Boy Amongst Men

Yfelde *see* Yfelde, John de
Kilwardby, Robert, archbishop of Canterbury (1273–78) 15, 79
Kingston, Dorset 97
Kirkby, John, bishop of Carlisle (1332–52) 4-5, 142
Kirkeby, William de 35
Knighton (chronicler) 34-5
Kyngesalre *see* Aller, church of

L

Lambeth:
 church of 125
 convocation at 92, 109 n. 1
Lanfranc, archbishop of Canterbury (1078–89) 1, 6 n. 1
Langdon Abbey, abbot of 37, 73, 81
Langham, Simon, abbot of Winchester, archbishop of Canterbury (1366–8) 9, 22 n. 4
Langton, John, bishop of Chichester (1305–37) 5, 15, 57 n. 22, 61, 68, 70, 72, 129, 137
 as chancellor of Edward I 11-12
Langton, Stephen, archbishop of Canterbury (1207–28) 2
lateran decrees 2
lawyer-bishops 22 n. 2
Le Deene (Richard), rector of Bremilham 100
Leeds Castle 38
Leeds Priory, Augustinian canons at 126
Leicester 34
Lenham, church of 64
Leveye (Leueye), Robert de 10, 75, 129
Lewes, archdeacon of (Thomas de Codelowe?) 73
Lewes Priory, prior of *see* Courtenay (Curtenay), John de, prior of Lewes, of Tavistock
Lewis of Bavaria 90
Lichfield, royal court at 14

Lincoln diocese 1-2, 4, 12, 14-15, 22 n. 2, 31, 70, 89-96, 98-9
 bishop of *see* Burghersh, Henry, bishop of Lincoln (1320–40)
Little Staughton, Bedfordshire 93
Llandaff Cathedral 10-11
Llandaff diocese 5, 142
London:
 Guildhall 30, 33
 house of Concoreto in 66, 72, 74
 Londoners in 30-1, 61
 Marshalsea prison 128 *see also* Makepays, Roger
 Old Temple 91
 provincial councils at *see* councils: provincial
 St. Paul's Cathedral (*see also* Fastolf, Laurence, canon of St. Paul's) 18, 32-3, 38, 61, 63, 87-8, 98-9, 114, 132
London diocese 40, 61
 bishop of *see* Gravesend, Stephen, bishop of London (1319–38)
 sede vacant composition for 54
Long Sutton, Somerset 95
Longbridge Deverill, Wiltshire 94
Lovell, Richard, patron of Northover 101
Luddenham, Kent 131
Lympne, rural dean of 73
Lyndwood, William 4
Lynn, Norfolk 10, 16, 30
Lyon, canonry of 89

M

Magna Carta 32, 34
Maidstone:
 church of 20, 125
 provision to 84
Makepays, Roger 128
Malling, woods at 49
Malling Abbey 126
Mancel, Thomas 68-9
Mankel, John 74

Mareschal, John le 35, 128
Marny (Maury), Richard, abbot of Milton (1331–52) 94
marriage 81
Martival, Roger, bishop of Salisbury (1315–30) 4, 58 n. 28, 101, 141
Mayfield 32, 77, 78 nn. 24, 28, 88, 90, 97-9, 114, 122, 133
  church of 21, 125
  manor of 75, 125
Melton, William, archbishop of York (1317–40) 4-5, 80-1, 89
Meopham 9-11
  historian of see Golding-Bird, C. H.
  indulgence for see Mepham, Simon (Symon) de, archbishop of Canterbury (1328–33): indulgence issued by
  parish records of 23 n. 11
Meopham, St. James de la Dene within parish of see St. James de la Dene, chantry in
Mepham, Edmund de (ob. 1329?) 10
  executor of see Leveye (Leueye), Robert de
Mepham, Edmund de (ob. 1333):
  as canon of Chichester, prebend of Llandaff 5, 10-11, 14, 22 n. 6, 22 n. 7, 25 n. 44, 47
  as official and vicar-general of the archbishop 15-17, 87
Mepham, Joan 10-11
Mepham, Richard de 11
Mepham, Simon (Symon) de, archbishop of Canterbury (1328–33) 4, 23 n. 16
  as canon of Chichester, prebendary of Llandaff 13
  consecration of 18, 59, 87, 89-90, 118, 125
  death and burial of 75
  early career of 8, 10-13
  early years of 9
  election to Canterbury of 13-14
  enthronement of 35-8
  indulgence issued by 22 n. 5, 23 n. 11, 100
  as prebend of Hova Villa 12
Mepham, Simon de, archdeacon of Salop 12

Mepham, Simon de, rector of Nuneham Courtenay 12
Mepham, Thomas de 10, 17, 25 n. 44
Mepham, William de, canon of Salisbury 11
Mereworth, John de 37
Middlesex, archbishop's manors in 21
Middleton, Richard de (clerk) 101
Middleton, Richard de (collation claimant) 92
Milsted, church of 97
Milton, church of 63
Milton Abbey 94 see also Marny (Maury), Richard, abbot of Milton (1331–52)
Minster, church of 63
Montfort, Simon de 11
Montgomery (Mont Gomery), John de 99
Mortimer, Roger, earl of March (1337) 6, 41 n. 4, 42 n. 11, 81, 85 n. 3
  regime with Isabella 28-31, 33-4, 41 n. 1, 80-1
Mortlake (archbishop's manor) 13, 25 n. 36, 88-95, 98-9, 115, 125, 129
Morton, Robert de, monk of Rochester 57 n. 18
Mota, Riamon de, commissary of Concoreto 98
Mundham, William de 97

N

Narcès, Armand de, archbishop of Aix-en-Provence 70, 136
Nassyngton, William de, canon of Exeter 73
Natyndon, Thomas de, monk of St. Augustine's 66, 68-9, 71, 135
Natyndon, William de, canon of Exeter 75, 99
Nederman, Cary J. 36
Neville, Edmund de 40, 90
New Sarum, Salisbury 30
Newark Priory 97
Newdegate (Newdigate) family 81

Archbishop Simon Mepham 1328-1333: A Boy Amongst Men

Newington, jurisdictional exemption of 98
Nicholas V, anti-pope (1328–30) *see* Corbaria, Peter (Petro) de
Norfolk 16, 30
North Waltham 98
Northampton 14
   Burghersh's summons of clergy to 115
   statute of 35
   treaty of 33-4
Northbourne, church of 64
Northburgh, Roger, bishop of Coventry and Lichfield (1322–58) 5, 109 n. 1, 140
Northfleet, Kent 11
Northover, Somerset 101
Norton, Wiltshire 100
Norwich 58 n. 34
Norwich Cathedral Priory 82
Norwich diocese, sede vacant composition for 54
Norwyco (Norwich), Walter de, monk of Canterbury 13
Nottingham 14
   castle at 25 n. 32
   provincial council at 1
Nuneham Courtenay 12 *see also* Mepham, Simon de, rector of Nuneham Courtenay

O

Offord, John de, archbishop of Canterbury (1348–49) 8-9, 79
Okeford Fitzpayne 51-2 *see also* Fitzpayne (Ftzpain), Ela
Old Temple *see* London: Old Temple
ordinations 11, 19-20, 26, 88, 97, 122
Orleton, Adam, bishop of Hereford (1317–27), of Worcester (1327–33), of Winchester (1333–45) 5, 19, 22 n. 2, 25 n. 31, 53, 60, 67, 70, 73, 76 n. 10, 79, 89–90, 93, 95, 116
Otford (archbishop's manor) 33, 80, 88-9, 91, 125

Oxenden, Richard de, prior of Canterbury 13, 20, 94, 97
Oxford (Oxonia), John de, monk of Rochester 57 n. 18
Oxford University 9, 11-12, 18, 22 n. 4, 23 n. 16, 109 n. 1

P

Pagula, William of 36, 43 n. 31
Palestrina, bishop of *see* Prés, Pierre de, cardinal bishop of Palestrina
parliaments 18, 30, 36, 40, 83, 91, 100, 115
   of Salisbury 30-1, 41, 88, 96
   of Westminster 41, 67, 76, 95-6
Paston, Benedict de 17
Patching, Essex 88
Payne, Ela la *see* Fitzpayne (Ftzpain), Ela
Pecham, John, archbishop of Canterbury (1279–92) 15, 37, 121-2
Penebrugg (Pembridge), John de 47
penitentiaries 20, 98
Percy, Henry de 69, 135 *see also* Petworth, Sussex
Peter, bishop of Corbavia *see* Corbavia (Corbaviensis), Peter de
Petworth, Sussex 69, 135
Philip VI, king of France 82
Philippa of Hainault, queen of Edward III 31, 38, 82, 91
pilgrimage 94, 99
Plumstead, visitation of church of 65
Pole, Richard de la 21
Poore, Richard, bishop of Chichester (1215–17), of Salisbury (1217–28), of Durham (1228–37) 2
Poterel, Geoffrey, monk of Canterbury 13-14
Poucy, Thomas Poucy, monk of St. Augustine's 66
Prés, Pierre de, cardinal bishop of Palestrina 15
Preston, church of 63, 76 n. 2

purgation 39-40, 49, 51, 69, 92
Pycard, Walter 65-6
Pynnore, William de 92, 132

Q

quadrennial tenth 92-4, 98-9

R

Ramsey Abbey, abbot of *see* Eye, Simon of, abbot of Ramsey
Registrum Actorum 17, 125
Renham, John de 18, 26, 38
Reynolds, Walter, bishop of Canterbury (1313–27) 4, 7, 11, 16-18, 23 n. 10, 37, 44 n. 34, 54, 55 n. 7, 59, 62, 77 n. 20, 131
  alleged illiteracy of 8, 14, 24 n. 30
  death of 13, 15, 28-9, 42 n. 17, 124
  silver chrismatorium of 122
Riddeswell, Robert 124
Rochester 16-17, 65-6, 97, 116, 119, 141
  visitation by Mepham of 46-7, 50 *see also* Hethe (Hythe), Hamo de, bishop of Rochester (1319–52)
Rochester Cathedral priory, visitation of 47-9
Roger, Edmund (of Higham) 37
Rogesio, Aymericus (Aymer) de, rector of St. Julian 67-8, 72, 76 n. 6, 76 n. 6, 137
Rome 1 *see also* Curia, Papal or Roman
Romsey abbey 87
Roscelyn, Thomas 34
Ross, John, bishop of Carlisle (1325–32) 4, 70
Rotherhithe, Surrey 53

S

St. Andrew, Hertford 88
St. Andrews, Scotland, archbishopric of 2
St. Andrew's Church, St. Mary's chantry in 99

St. Augustine's Abbey 46, 54, 71-2, 74
  appropriated churches of 65
St. Augustine's Abbey, Mepham's visitation of 39, 50, 63-4, 68, 100
St. Giles chapel 89-90
St. James de la Dene, chantry in 11, 23 n. 10
St. Julian, rector of *see* Rogesio, Aymericus (Aymer) de, rector of St. Julian
St. Leonard's Church 89
St. Nicholas Church 49
St. Radegund's (Bradsole) Abbey 37
St. Thomas the Martyr, College of 60
Salisbury, parliament at *see* parliaments: of Salisbury
Salisbury Cathedral 50-3
  song school close to 51
Salisbury diocese 50-2, 94-7
  bishops of:
    Ghent *see* Ghent (Gandavo), Simon of, bishop of Salisbury (1297-1315)
    Martival *see* Martival, Roger, bishop of Salisbury (1315-30)
    Poore *see* Poore, Richard, bishop of Chichester (1215-17), of Salisbury (1217-28), of Durham (1228-37)
    Wyville *see* Wyville (Wyvil), Robert, bishop of Salisbury (1330-75)
  sede vacante composition of *see* sede vacante compositions
  visitation of 100-1
Salmon, John, bishop of Norwich (1299–1325) 54
Salop, archdeaconry of 11-12
Sancta Margareta, Hugh de, sacrist of Christ Church 121
Sancto Petro, Simon de, monk of Canterbury 13
Sandwich, rural dean of 73
Sapiti, Andreas (Andrea) 75, 77 n. 23
Sarlat diocese 76 n. 6, 137
Scots, war with 33, 99
Scottish sees 2 *see also* Galloway (Whithorn; Candida Casa), bishopric of

sede vacante compositions 21, 50, 53, 64, 75, 82, 92-3
sees 2, 4, 22, 50, 53, 82, 140
Shalford, Surrey 93
Shipton Moyne, Henry de, vicar of Norton 100
Shoreditch (Schordich; Schorditch; Schordwich), John de 66, 76 n. 7
Shoreham (Shorham), William de 23 n. 11, 23, 82, 100
Shrewsbury, Ralph of, bishop of Bath and Wells (1329–63) 18, 26 n. 47, 44 n. 37, 57 n. 22, 73, 89-90, 92, 95-6, 140
  dispensation for pilgrimage of 94
Skirlaw, William, bishop of Durham (1388–1406) 6
Slindon (archbishop's manor) 68-70, 83, 93-4, 125, 134-7
Smarden, Kent 38
Sodbury, Adam of, abbot of Glastonbury (1323–34) 37
South Malling, Kent 16
Southampton, sheriff of 31
Southwark 53, 60
Speculum Regis 36, 43
Speldhurst, John de, prior of Rochester (1321–33) 56 n. 15
Stalbridge (Stapelbrigg), Dorset 100 *see also* Wyville (Wyvil), Robert, bishop of Salisbury (1330–75)
Stamford, Council of (1327) 13
Stapeldon, Walter, bishop of Exeter (1308–26) 33, 60-1, 114
Stoke, N. de 101
Stratford, John:
  as archbishop of Canterbury (1333–48) 8, 16, 18, 38, 55 n. 1, 82, 109, 116
    provincial constitutions of 4, 6 n. 11
    as royal chancellor 5, 81
    sermons of 23 n. 16
Strood catalogue 23
Strood Hospital 49
Sturry, church of 63

Surrey:
  archbishop's manors in 21
  archdeaconry of 60
Sussex, archbishop's manors in 21
Swaneslond (Swonlond), Simon de 81
Swinfield, Richard de, bishop of Hereford (1283–1317) 11

T

Tarrant Monkton 96
Tarring, deanery of 88
Tenterden, church of 64
Teynham:
  archbishop's manor in 38
  church of 125
  vicarage of 88
Thames (river) 9, 16, 87, 119
Thorne (Thorn), William, monk of St. Augustine's 46, 55 nn. 2, 4
Tonbridge:
  barony of 37
  lord of *see* Clare, Gilbert de, earl de Gloucester (ob. 1314)
Totnes, archdeacon of 60
treasurers:
  archiepiscopal 18
  royal 5
Trottiscliffe:
  bishop's manor in 32, 75
  church of 125
Trussell, William 34
Tunstall, Hamo de 75
Tunstall, Kent 11

U

Upchurch, parish of 130

V

Viannde, Roberto 120
visitations 38-9, 45-50, 53-4, 64-5, 68,

90-1, 94-7
Viventius, Bernard, canon of St. Emilion 73

W

Wake, Thomas 30, 33-4
Waltham, Essex 34
Waltham Abbey, abbot of *see* Hertford, Richard de, abbot of Waltham (1308–45)
Waltham Chase 31
Warwick 34, 147
Waverley, Surrey 95
Weald, the 56
Wells Cathedral, visitation of 50, 94-5
West Monkton 95
Westbere, rural dean of 39, 73
Westerham, John de, prior of Rochester (1320–21) 56 n. 15
Westminster:
  exchequer at 12
  parliament at 41 n. 4, 67, 76, 95-6
  royal palace at 82, 91
Westminster Abbey 19, 22 n. 4, 82
  abbots of:
    Curlington *see* Curtlington, William de, abbot of Westminster
    Langham *see* Langham, Simon, abbot of Winchester, archbishop of Canterbury (1366-8)
Weston, Robert de 26 n. 45, 48
  as auditor of causes 18, 38-9, 124-7
  makes Mepham's funeral arrangements 75
Wharton, Henry 55 nn. 2, 4
Wickhambreux, church of 96
Winchelsey, Robert, archbishop of Canterbury (1294–1313) 4, 11, 16-17, 25 n. 42, 37, 64, 89
  bible of 122
  gloves and other items of 121
  statutes of 109 n. 1
Winchester:
  archdeaconry of 60
  bishops of 51, 60, 67, 91, 98
  convocation at 91
  Lancastrian forces gather at 31-2, 34
  parliament at 91
  diocese of 41, 52-3, 91, 93, 95, 97-8
Windsor 89
Windsor, John de 17
Windsor, Ralph de 17
Wingham:
  archbishop's manor at 82, 86 n. 8, 89, 93
  church of 125
  provost of 88
Wither, Sir Thomas 34
Wittersham 16, 89 *see also* Woodhouse, John de, rector of Wittersham
Wiveliscombe, Somerset 50-1, 96-7, 101
Woghope (Wouhope), Thomas de, rector of Smarden 16, 38, 71, 97, 120
  as Mepham's executor 38
  as warden of the archbishop's chapel 16, 121
Woodhouse, John de, rector of Wittersham 89
Woodstock, Edmund of, earl of Kent 30-5, 42 n. 11, 43 n. 27, 81, 85 n. 5
Woodstock, John de, monk of Rochester 49
Worcester 30, 34
  royal forces at 34
Worcester diocese 15, 17, 22 n. 2, 141
  bishop of 53, 60, 67, 70, 73
  sede vacante composition for 54
Wormedal, Nicolaum de, monk of Boxley 131
Worth, Robert de, canon of Salisbury 92
Wright, Thomas, incumbent of Meopham (1742–63) 23 n. 11
Wrotenham (Wrotham), Peter de 74
Wrotham church 125
Wylie (Wyle), Nicholas de la 100
Wylie (Wyle), Richard de la, rector of Hawkchurch 100
Wylie (Wyle), William de la, rector of Stalbridge 100
Wymundham, John de 99
Wyvelesberg, Thomas 66

Wyville (Wyvil), Robert, bishop of
Salisbury (1330–75) 5-6, 21, 51, 57 n.
22, 58 n. 28, 70, 92, 98-9, 141

Y

Yfelde, John de 40
Yford, Laurence de 65-6
York:
 parliament at 30
 province of 1-2, 4, 95-6
York diocese 1, 70
 primatial cross 91, 93

Printed in Great Britain
by Amazon